MAXIMILIAN KOLBE

Saint of Auschwitz

✝

FUNDS TO PURCHASE
THIS BOOK WERE
PROVIDED BY A
40TH ANNIVERSARY GRANT
FROM THE
FOELLINGER FOUNDATION.

KOLBE

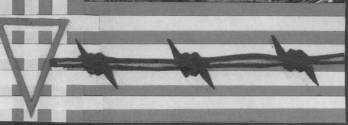

Maximilian Kolbe
Saint of Auschwitz

BY

ELAINE MURRAY STONE

ILLUSTRATED BY

PATRICK KELLEY

PAULIST PRESS
NEW YORK/MAHWAH, N.J.

Cover design by James F. Brisson.

Illustrations are by Patrick Kelley.

Note on frontispiece: Original art courtesy of Ted Wojtkowski,
author of the Foreword.

Library of Congress Cataloging-in-Publication Data

Stone, Elaine Murray, 1922–
    Maximilian Kolbe : Saint of Auschwitz / by Elaine Murray Stone.
        p.   cm.
    Includes bibliographical references.
    Summary: A biography of the Polish friar. canonized in 1982, who
founded the Militia of the Immaculate, wrote numerous periodicals
and newspapers, and while imprisoned in Auschwitz, sacrificed his
life for another man.
    ISBN 0-8091-6637-2 (alk. paper)
    1. Kolbe, Maximilian, Saint, 1894–1941—Juvenile literature.
2. Christian saints—Poland—Biography—Juvenile literature.
[1. Kolbe, Maximilian, Saint, 1894–1941.   2. Saints.]   I. Title.
BX4700.K55S86 1997
282'.092—dc21
[b]
                                                        96-46700
                                                            CIP
                                                            AC

Published by Paulist Press
997 Macarthur Boulevard
Mahwah, New Jersey 07430

Printed and bound in the
United States of America

CONTENTS

PREFACE / *vii*

FOREWORD / *xi*

1 Childhood Years / *1*

2 School and Seminary / *10*

3 A Prayer Is Answered / *23*

4 A City for Mary / *36*

5 In Japan / *46*

6 Return to Niepokalanow / *55*

7 The Occupation of Poland / *65*

8 In the Death Camp:
May 28-August 14, 1941 / *74*

9 It Is Finished / *85*

10 A Saint for Poland / *95*

BIBLIOGRAPHY / *106*

PREFACE

No author can write the life story of another person without doing lots of research and making contacts to get special information and see the places associated with the subject. St. Maximilian Kolbe has had a hold on my heart for many years. In 1990 I won a national award for an essay I wrote about him. This award spurred my interest in learning more about his life. After accumulating a pile of books about the saint's life, I set to work writing what eventually became this manuscript. But as I progressed, I sensed something was missing in it. Besides, I had found many inconsistencies among the books I read. It was time to go to the source and straighten things out. I decided to visit Poland.

There would have been no trip and no contacts if not for my Polish friends in Melbourne Beach, Florida, Donna and John Czarnecki. When they learned of my interest in St. Maximilian Kolbe, they contacted friends in Lodz, Poland, which culminated in my receiving an invitation to visit there.

So, in August of 1995, I flew to Warsaw where I was met by Kasia Galant and Krystyna Skolska. They drove me to the home of my hosts, Mary and Kos Zuk in Lagiewniki.

After dinner at their home, they said I had been invited to stay at the nearby monastery of St. Anthony for the entire week of my visit.

With this ancient Franciscan monastery as my base, I traveled every day to different places associated with St. Maximilian: Zdunska Wola, Pabianice, Niepokalanow, Czestochowa, Auschwitz and later Cracow. I met several friars who had known St. Maximilian, as well as the saint's eighty-seven year old first cousin, Bronislawa Papuzinska, who told me much about Maximilian's childhood.

In the refectory of St. Anthony's in Lagiewniki, I sat every day at meals beside Fr. Peter Mielczaker. He had been Fr. Kolbe's private secretary at Niepokalanow during the years 1936 to 1939 and told me stories of the saint's goodness.

Many people helped me during my stay, none more so than Fr. George Domanski, O.F.M. Conv., the world's leading authority on the life of St. Maximilian Kolbe. In addition to taking me on a private tour of the Kolbe Museum at Niepokalanow, he kept my manuscript a week, making extensive suggestions and corrections. Kolbe had been one of this friar's professors in the seminary. For the past fifty years, Fr. Domanski has been editor of *The Knight*, which has a present circulation of 700,000 issues per month. Also, from 1975 to 1985, he was international director of the Knights of the Immaculate, numbering three million members.

I am most deeply indebted to Kasia Galant, a young student majoring in English at Lodz University, who not only drove me all over Poland but acted as my interpreter throughout my stay.

My thanks go to Mary and Kos Zuk for their wonderful hospitality, and also to Krystyna and Bogdan Skolska.

Krystyna is the famous artist who sculptured the huge bronze statues of St. Maximilian at Niepokalanow, Zdunska Wola and Pabianice. Utilizing all her connections with Franciscan Friars, Sisters of St. Maximilian, and priests, she was able to open doors for me everywhere.

My deepest gratitude goes to the friars at St. Anthony's in Lagiewniki outside Lodz for the loving, joyful care they offered to the "writer lady" in their midst, and in particular to Fr. Joseph Makarczyk, who was the perfect host and example of Franciscan hospitality.

My heartfelt gratitude goes to Ted Wojtkowski of Skokie, Illinois, for writing his deeply moving Foreword for this book.

I naturally want to thank my editor, Karen Scialabba, who was instrumental in getting this book through many phases to publication. Her suggestions and patience have added so much to that particular relationship known only to writers with their editors.

My hope is that many adults and children will come to know St. Maximilian Kolbe through my book and will try to follow this example of perfect love.

—ELAINE MURRAY STONE

FOREWORD

Never, never would I have dreamed that I would be so fortunate as to witness the moment when a new saint was born! (O Lord, I am ashamed of my own weakness.)

When Fr. Kolbe sacrificed his own life for one of our fellow prisoners, I stood frozen with fear and begged God for my own life.

I was in my early twenties when the world collapsed around me very suddenly. The Second World War marked the beginning of such horrible deeds. Then I found myself in a man-made hell with the unusual name of Auschwitz (Polish: Oswiecim), which may be translated properly and ironically as "Enlightenment." Exactly during the time when most of the killings occurred in the concentration camp, God placed his hand at the bottom of this hell and pointed out very clearly that only love is victorious.

The saint's own sacrifice was the sign of this victory.

It occurred as I was undergoing my third "selection," a punishment meted out to prisoners whenever a fellow prisoner was missing. The first time we called it "Wiejowski Night." A prisoner named "Wiejowski" had escaped from the camp through the sewer system. For punishment everyone had to stand at attention for two days without food or water. After about six months, he was caught, brought back to Auschwitz and executed.

At the second "selection," when a second prisoner escaped, ten innocent prisoners were chosen at random and were immediately cut down by machine guns!

At the third "selection," I was standing behind Fr. Kolbe; he was in the sixth row and I was standing in the eighth row. I experienced a strange feeling that I was standing on the edge between life and death. With my eyes closed, I prayed, "O Lord, please make them select anybody else, but save my life!" Suddenly I opened my eyes and feverishly began to count how many prisoners had already been selected. My last hope was that perhaps the guard already had selected ten before they reached my row. But I counted only six.

As the commandant approached from the right side between the fifth and sixth rows, one of the men already selected started to cry out, "Oh, my children, my wife!" At that same moment, Fr. Kolbe stepped out in front of the commandant and expressed his wish to be substituted for the father of the children.

"You must be some kind of crazy priest," said Fritsch, the commandant, in wonder.

Then he called out loudly, "Exchange!" And the two prisoners changed places.

I looked at Fr. Kolbe's face—so peaceful, so serene. His altruistic act inspired me for the rest of my life.

I firmly believe that at the most tragic moments of our lives, God creates some saints among us to enlighten us so that we ask ourselves: "Who am I? Do I love my neighbor as much as myself?"

St. Maximilian Kolbe, through his heroic act, is the best proof of my firm belief.

Ted Wojtkowski, Ex-Prisoner of Auschwitz, No. 339

Maximilian Kolbe

Saint of Auschwitz

✝

CHAPTER ONE

CHILDHOOD YEARS

A Rambunctious Boy

"Raymond, go fetch the switch!" snapped Maria. The boy's mother was beside herself with all the trouble he kept getting into. Her son Raymond was full of energy and curiosity. Both kept him in disgrace at home.

Obediently, the eight year old boy, one day to be known as St. Maximilian Kolbe, ran with the switch to his overworked mother. He bent over the bench as Maria gave him another in a long series of thrashings.

Maria Dabrowska was the nineteenth century equivalent of a modern working mother. She and her husband Julius were domestic weavers, as were most of the workers in their town of Zdunska Wola. They bought bushels of yarn. Then they sat at their looms all day and far into the night, weaving cloth to sell to the merchants in nearby Lodz.

As hard as they worked, Julius and Maria could never get ahead. They had barely enough food for their little boys. The entire family lived in one room on the second floor of a frame cottage. Three other families each occupied other rooms. The looms were in a room on the ground floor.

Zdunska Wola lay in the center of Poland, an area governed by Russia. Between 1772 and 1815, Poland was divided into three zones. The area lived in by the Kolbes was under the harsh rule of Czar Nicholas II. Pressure was put on Polish Catholics to speak Russian and to give their allegiance to the czar. Catholic convents were closed and nuns were forbidden to wear habits. Maria and Julius continued to live as devout Catholics, attending daily mass at their nearby church. They were even members of the Third Order of St. Francis, a rule for lay persons.

His Parents Meet

During her teens Maria had dreamed of becoming a nun, but it was not possible at that time as all the convents had been closed. Then along came the serious young patriot, Julius Kolbe. Maria's parents were thrilled when he began courting their daughter. Maria and Julius were married in the Church of the Assumption in Zdunska Wola on October 5, 1891.

Their first son was born a year later. They named him Francis in honor of their patron saint. The baby slept in a wooden cradle beside their big double bed. The only other furniture in their one room apartment was a wooden table and chairs and their marriage chest.

In a corner stood a ceramic stove for heat. A small shrine to the Virgin Mary was set up behind a privacy curtain. Red votive candles flickered before it all day. Here the devout couple knelt together to recite their morning and evening prayers.

With the birth of Francis, Maria was busier than ever, nursing her infant son and working many hours at the loom downstairs. Two years later on January 8, 1894, the future saint was born. They named him Raymond, his aunt taking him to be baptized the day of his birth at the nearby church where his parents had been married.

Three more sons were born to the Kolbes, Joseph in 1896, Walenty in 1897, and Anthony in 1900. Walenty lived only a year.

Raymond turned out to be a bundle of energy, curiosity and boisterousness. He was into everything. Over and over his exhausted mother wailed, "Raymie, Raymie, whatever will become of you?" After baby Walenty died, the Kolbes suffered another loss. Raymond was ten when his beloved little brother Anthony died at the age of four. He had loved cherubic Anthony very much, and the loss hurt him deeply. Now there remained only three boys.

Julius realized that his meager income would never stretch enough to clothe, feed and educate his three remaining sons. Maria wondered if there was anything she could do to improve their lot. How could they escape such grueling poverty?

A New City

In time she discovered a way to increase the family income. First, the Kolbes moved to the larger city of Pabianice where Maria often helped the poor as a midwife. With a little training she began delivering babies, often donating her services. Then she opened a shop in part of their rented house where she sold household goods and groceries.

Julius went to work in the nearby Krusche and Ender mill, a huge factory that made cloth by machine. He also rented a plot of land where he raised vegetables to sell at the local market.

Julius even found time to play with his growing boys. In the winter he raced his sons barefoot through the snow. It was part of his health-building regimen. A Polish patriot, Julius was involved in the illegal Resistance. As a result the Kolbe boys were interested in everything military. The boys built play forts and marched around with sticks for guns. Their enemy was always the army of Nicholas II, their Russian ruler. But this could be dangerous and incur the wrath of the Russian authorities.

School Days

For their education the boys went to the parish priest. He taught them catechism and a smattering of Latin. Maria had already taught them to read at home. Fr. Vladimir Jakowski quickly noted the bright mind of his student Raymond. Here was a boy who deserved a fine education. But how could his family manage it? They barely had enough money for food and rent.

But as the Kolbe family's income increased, Julius felt they could afford to send at least one son to school. Francis, the oldest, was enrolled at the local industrial, or trade school. There wasn't enough money to send Raymond, too. Maria put Raymond to work in her store where he helped with sales and keeping the books. Then one day something happened that changed the course of his life.

An Egg Causes Trouble

Some of Raymond's friends had pets. One owned a dog, another had a canary. Raymond yearned for a pet, too! But his mother said they couldn't afford such a luxury. One day Raymond used one of the family's zlotys to buy a hen egg. He planned to hatch it and start a business.

The youngster placed his egg under a nesting chicken in a neighbor's hen house.

Tending it carefully, Raymond looked forward to the moment when it would break out of its shell and provide him with the pet he craved. But he hadn't counted on the neighbor's friendship with his mother.

One morning the neighbor came over for a visit. "Mrs. Kolbe," she whined, "that naughty son of yours has been up to no good. I've seen him sneaking in and out of our hen house!"

"My Raymond!" gasped Maria, acting surprised although she was prepared to hear almost anything about her head-strong boy. "And what do you suppose he is up to in your hen house?" asked Maria, wiping her sweaty hands on her snowy white apron in embarrassment. She tried not to show her concern.

"Yes, of course it was Raymond. No one else," the neighbor replied in an accusing tone.

"Well, I'll ask him," agreed the red-faced mother. "Let's find out right now."

"Raymond!" she called. "Raymond! Come here this minute!" The young boy came running, his clogs hammering on the wooden floor. "Yes, Mother," he puffed.

"What have you been up to, sneaking into Mrs. Zaleska's hen house?"

Raymond peered up at the two puzzled women. He had been taught both at home and in catechism class to always tell the truth.

"Nothing, really," he replied, blushing to the roots of his brown hair.

"Nothing!" snapped his mother, getting angrier by the second. "What kind of nothing? I want a straight answer." She glanced threateningly toward the birch switch on the wall.

Finally Raymond raised his deep brown eyes, brimming with tears. One trickled down his cheek. "Mother, I'm sorry. I wanted a pet. You know how much St. Francis loved birds. I wanted a chicken of my own."

"What chicken?" grimaced Maria. "We don't have chickens."

"Well, it's not one yet. But it will be soon. You'll see. I bought an egg and placed it under Mrs. Zaleska's laying hen. I expected the chicken to hatch it along with her other eggs."

"You bought an egg?" shrilled Maria. "With what? My food money? The zlotys I've been saving for Christmas?" She glowered down at the repentant youngster. "You bad boy. Bring me that switch. Whatever will become of you?"

A Turning Point

Maria proceeded to give poor Raymond the beating of his life. But his painful punishment and his mother's tearful reproach bore fruit. It was a turning point in his life. Raymond began disappearing behind the curtain to kneel at the family altar. On it was a statue of Our Lady of Czestochowa. Sometimes Maria could hear him sighing and weeping.

Maria never had to use the switch again. Something deep and mysterious had come over Raymond. Her son had become a model boy.

Eventually Maria could no longer contain her curiosity about his change. One day she asked Raymond what had prompted his sudden, deep interest in religion. What was it about?

The Vision

Raymond seemed embarrassed to reveal his secret. But finally, shaking with emotion, he obeyed and told her. "One day, when I was praying before the painting of Our Lady of Czestochowa in church," he began softly, "Our Lady appeared to me."

Maria's broad face looked shocked. Could this be true, or was her son being sacrilegious? Even worse, perhaps he was going crazy. But she nodded for Raymond to continue.

"Our Lady was holding out two crowns. One was white, the other red. She gazed at me lovingly and asked, `Which of these crowns do you desire?' Then the Virgin told me that if I chose the white crown I would remain pure for life. The red one was a martyr's crown. I thought about the choice for a minute. Then I told her, 'I want both of them.' The Virgin smiled sweetly at me. Then she disappeared."

As he spoke, Raymond's face glowed with peace and innocence. His mother could not help believing what he told her. But the greatest proof of the vision was the immediate change in her son's behavior. Obviously, something miraculous had taken place and transformed him.

They Make a Pilgrimage

It was the custom of the Kolbe family to make a pilgrimage each year in August to the Holy Shrine of the Virgin of Czestochowa. They wanted to arrive there in time for the feast of the Assumption on August 15. Days before leaving on the hundred mile pilgrimage, Maria would take out her husband's only suit to air it out and brush it. She washed and ironed her young sons' Sunday shirts. Finally, she packed food for their long journey—bread, cheese and sausage.

Each year hundreds of thousands of devout Poles left homes and traveled by foot, wagon or train to visit the shrine of the Black Madonna. The image of the Madonna was painted sometime between the years 500 and 800. The painting had turned black after centuries of smoke and wax from all the candles placed before it.

History of the Famous Image

The painting was brought to the monastery of Jasna Gora by Prince Ladislaus Opaczyk in 1384. Jasna Gora is a fortress monastery high on a hill overlooking the city of Czestochowa. The image shows Mary pointing her index finger at the infant Jesus seated on her lap.

In 1492 the first miracle of healing took place at Jasna Gora after a sick person prayed in front of the painting. As more miracles occurred, hundreds, then thousands of pilgrims journeyed to pray before the famous Black Madonna. She became known as the Healer of the Sick, Mother of Mercy, and Queen of Poland.

Kings, princes, knights, and simple peasants traveled great distances to pray for health or success in battle. Pope John Paul II made many pilgrimages to Czestochowa as a young priest, and later as head of the Roman Catholic Church.

In the sixteenth century, King Ladislaus ordered that the heads of the mother and child be crowned in pure gold.

Today, with the iron curtain ripped away, as many as a million pilgrims from all over the world gather in the fields below the monastery. On the feast of the Assumption, they sing hymns, praise God, and ask for the Madonna's help.

On the Way

Maria Kolbe began preparing a month ahead for her family's annual pilgrimage. They were joined on the way by other devout families until there was a great crowd making their way to Jasna Gora. As they walked through the countryside of rich fields and dark forests, Raymond's thoughts were drawn to the goodness of God in creating such abundance and beauty. Often his heart was full at the thought of how the Holy Virgin had even come to visit him. Would she ever speak to him again? Would she be there at Czestochowa? He wondered aloud, "How can I show my great love for her?"

"Raymond," his mother's voice drew him from his reverie. "We are stopping here for lunch. Here is some bread and cheese." Raymond took the food, thanking her with his soft voice and sweet smile. Then he glanced around at the pilgrims, resting on the ground and eating with them. There were women with pink cheeks and brightly colored scarves, mothers in the traditional peasant costume, babies wrapped in swaddling cloths, carefree boys and girls in their Sunday best darting about, racing and playing tag, and fathers in shiny black suits. All were excited about the trip and the possibility of seeing a miracle.

CHAPTER TWO

SCHOOL AND SEMINARY

A Special Errand

Raymond returned from their annual pilgrimage to work in the family store. From time to time his mother sent him on errands.

One day, when Raymond was nearly twelve, Maria needed a poultice for a woman having a difficult delivery. She sent Raymond to the pharmacy for it, saying, "Ask Doc Kotowski for some *vencon greca*. He will know what it is. And here's the money." She put some coins in his palm.

Ever since his vision of the Holy Virgin, Raymond had been quick to obey. He ran past the graveyard near their house and across town. Arriving out of breath, Raymond politely removed his cap and asked the pharmacist, "Please, sir, may I have some *vencon greca*? My mother, Maria Kolbe, needs it right away."

Surprised at the boy's perfect pronunciation of the medical term, he asked, "Where did you learn Latin, my boy?"

"Sir, I've been studying it with Fr. Jakowski," replied

Raymond. "Besides, my mother has to know Latin terms. She's a midwife, you know."

"Of course, of course," mumbled the pharmacist. "And are you planning to be a doctor someday?" he asked, pounding the poultice with his mortar and pestle.

"Oh, no, sir!" exclaimed Raymond, smiling brightly. "I want to be a priest!"

Rather surprised by the answer, the man handed Raymond an envelope with the powder, adding, "Now run along to your mother."

How a Pharmacist Helped Raymond

The pharmacist didn't forget the incident. He knew that the Kolbes could never afford to send all three boys away to school. Seminary study took years, and hardly anyone could pay for it. But Raymond seemed such a bright, sincere lad. "If given half a chance," the pharmacist scratched his chin, "Raymond would make a fine priest." Doc Kotowski decided to do something about it.

One Sunday the pharmacist dropped by the Kolbe house, where he found Maria alone. After the usual greetings and being invited to take a seat on one of the family's hard benches, he said, "Mrs. Kolbe, your middle son, Raymond, is a very bright boy." Maria beamed with pride. The kindly man continued, "I understand that he has hopes of becoming a priest."

Maria nodded, "Yes. Unfortunately, for him, it is only a dream." She twisted her apron in embarrassment. "Doctor, we don't have the funds for such a long, expensive education. Besides, Raymond is behind in school. I have kept him home to help me in the store."

"My dear Mrs. Kolbe," smiled the pharmacist, "take heart. Here, let me propose something to you. Suppose I tutor Raymond in Latin so that he can catch up. In mathematics, too, if he needs it."

Maria threw up her hands in protest. "But..." she stammered, "you know we cannot pay."

"No, no. You don't understand. I am offering to teach your son for nothing. He deserves it. He is a bright, hard-working lad."

Maria's eyes glanced toward the spot on the wall where the switch had hung for so many years. Somehow, it was true. Her troublesome boy had become a model youngster, quiet and serious. She nodded her head. "Yes, my Raymond would do very well. All he needs is some help."

"I am offering you that help," smiled the pharmacist, rising to leave.

From then on, every day after work, Raymond rushed off to study with Doc Kotowski. Raymond proved himself to be a dedicated hard-working student. By the end of the year, he had caught up with his older brother. Then something unexpected happened to both Raymond and Francis.

A Wonderful Offer

During Lent in the spring of 1907, a group of Franciscan friars from the Austrian zone of Poland came to Pabianice to conduct a mission. On the last evening, Fr. Jakowski announced that the friars were opening a school and seminary in Lwow. "They will train young boys and men for the priesthood and possibly to serve as missionaries. All tuition, room and board, will be provided free of charge!"

Raymond could hardly believe his ears. Everything would

be free! Now he could be a priest after all. At the close of the service, Raymond and his older brother Francis rushed to the sacristy. Explaining their situation, they begged the friars to accept them at the new school.

Raymond was told he would have to take a test to prove he was ready. Because the kind pharmacist had helped Raymond with Latin and math, he was able to pass easily. Then came prayers and letters and applications to be filled out.

Off to School

Finally, both boys were enrolled. In August of 1907, Raymond and Francis boarded the train for Lwow. So that they could pass the border with ease, their father had dressed them in Austrian-looking suits and suggested that they not say anything in Polish. Maria stood weeping into her handkerchief as the train puffed its way out of the station. Now, only her youngest boy, Joseph, would be at home. Suddenly her life felt empty and the little cottage seemed almost too big.

As expected, Raymond was an excellent scholar. He quickly picked up the German language, which was used almost exclusively in the community where the school was located. Later it would come in handy. He also excelled in math and science, not at all what his parents had expected of their devout son. In his senior year Raymond drew blueprints for a space ship, and showed interest in military strategy, making plans for a battlement for Lwow. He even considered enlisting in the army. But he put his best efforts into his religious studies.

A Big Decision

Raymond was only sixteen when he was required to make a major decision. If he wanted to continue at the seminary and be ordained, he would have to give up marriage and a family forever. He must also promise to enter the Franciscan Order immediately to begin the novitiate. It seemed too much to give up.

Raymond decided to talk this over with his older brother, Francis, who had already made up his mind to enter the Order and become a priest. Raymond told him, "Francis, this really isn't the life for me. I like math and science. I would do better as an inventor, or in the military."

"If that's how you feel about being a friar," Francis said, "we must go immediately and tell the Father Superior. It would be wrong to keep this from him." Francis was gravely disappointed about Raymond's decision.

A Lucky Visit

The brothers were walking down the hall to the Superior's office when a friar stopped them. "Boys, your mother is here to see you. She is waiting in the visitors' parlor." Hearing that, they bolted down the stairs to greet her.

Maria grabbed them, exclaiming, "Raymond! Francis! Let me look at you. How tall you are!"

She held the self-conscious teenagers at arm's length, admiring their black cassocks and short hair. Then Maria sat down to share her exciting news. "My dear boys, your brother Joseph has decided to follow you into the Franciscan Order. Isn't that wonderful! Can you imagine such joy, giving all of my sons to serve the Lord? Joseph will be entering here as soon as he is old enough."

Stunned, Raymond looked at Francis, while Francis grinned in triumph. There was no way Raymond could leave now. Joseph would be too disappointed. Besides, he would be letting down his mother.

Mrs. Kolbe Makes a Change

But Maria's next sentence came as a shock. "Now that all our children will soon be out of the nest," she said excitedly, "your father and I have decided to follow our original dream. Papa has already left for Cracow to live near the Franciscan monastery there. I plan to move here to Lwow with Joseph and live near the Benedictine nuns. Joseph will come with me to attend St. Casimir's. It's a nice boarding school not far from here."

God had moved in the hearts of all five Kolbes and drawn them to his service. That year the little cottage and store were closed. The Kolbes' few belongings were given to the poor. Julius and Maria would have no further use for them.

The Novitiate

On September 4, 1910, Raymond was admitted as a novice in the Franciscan Order. He chose "Maximilian Maria" as his name in religion. Maximilian was the name of an early Christian saint, as well as of an emperor of Austria. Now known as "Brother Maximilian," he was clothed in the black habit with its cowl. A white cord with three knots, denoting poverty, chastity and obedience, was tied around his waist. But this was just the first step in a long process before he would be fully professed and ordained. Besides, he still had another year of the seminary to complete.

The first leg of this journey began with his entrance into

the novitiate. He was happy to be a part of the great Order founded by St. Francis. Maximilian did everything to live like that saint. He was constantly praying and fasting.

Scruples Get in the Way

Unfortunately, this noble goal caused him to be attacked by fears of unworthiness. He felt urged to do more, to pray more. It seemed to him that everything he did was wrong, or not worthy of his vocation. Eventually these attacks of scruples made him ill.

To help him, his roommate, Bronislaus Stryczny, suggested, "You should report to me whenever you are attacked by scruples. Just sharing such temptations with another will send Satan running." The young students made a vow together. "We will pray for each other daily until the end of our lives," said Maximilian. "If one dies first, the other will keep the promise until we meet in heaven."

The Move to Cracow

In 1912 Maximilian was sent to Cracow for further studies. He had taken his first vows as a friar. Cracow was two hundred miles from his former home in Pabianice and was the third largest city in Poland. Like Lwow, it was an ancient university town renowned for its culture and learning. Ornate towers of its cathedral rose above the skyline. Considered the most beautiful city in Poland, it was once the capital.

There the serious young friar struggled with the deep questions of life, in both philosophy and theology.

On the huge town square stood St. Mary Queen of Heaven, the most famous church in the country. It had two towers of different heights, the tallest circled by a golden crown to honor the Blessed Virgin, Poland's patron.

Maximilian must have visited Cracow's beautiful churches many times to admire them and to pray. Beneath the ancient cathedral lay the tomb of St. Stanislaus, the first Pole to be canonized in 1253. In this building of spires and colorful stained glass were the tombs of many kings who had once ruled Poland.

Maximilian did not remain long in that center of churches and history. His quick mind and love of study attracted the attention of the faculty and their Father Superior, and as a result Maximilian was selected to continue his studies for the priesthood in Rome. What a great honor for a young man from far-off Poland!

Not What He Wanted

Anyone else might have been thrilled to live near the Vatican and the holy father, where so many early Christians had been martyred for their faith. But in 1912, Rome was also renowned as a city of sin. Still troubled by scruples, Maximilian felt that he might lose his purity in such a den of iniquity. Surrounded by so many worldly delights, he feared that he might yield to temptation. But as an obedient Franciscan, Maximilian accepted the will of his Superior. When he was ordered to go to Rome, he obeyed.

The capital of Italy was a sprawling, sophisticated city, covering seven hills. The Vatican was only a small independent state within it, having its own laws, traditions and guards. By Italian law, the Pope was not allowed to travel outside its walls, making him a veritable prisoner in Vatican City.

Off to Rome

In October of 1912, Maximilian left Poland to study at the International Seraphic College in Rome. His professors were often stumped by Maximilian's questions regarding science and religion. Maximilian also studied philosophy at the Gregorian University which was run by the Jesuits. But something besides getting excellent grades fired Maximilian's mind.

While in the Eternal City, Maximilian was drawn more and more to revere and honor the Virgin Mary. He had already seen her in his vision; now he felt her presence in everything he undertook. The young friar yearned to be her champion, dedicated as medieval knights were to the lady of their heart. He pledged that his life would be as pure and immaculate as hers.

A Popular Student

All the students grew to love the smiling, thoughtful young man. A whiz at math, he tutored those who were slower. Anytime a fellow student felt down, he would comfort him: "Next time everything will be all right." Maximilian loved fruit for dessert. But whenever it was served, he gave his portion to a friend.

He also loved chess and became an expert at the game. His ability at math, and his interest in military maneuvers easily made him the college champion.

All through the four bloody years of World War I, as millions of other young men were dying on the battlefields of Europe, Maximilian was safely studying in Rome. He was uncomfortably aware, however, that cities were being shelled, soldiers were dying in muddy trenches and civilians were displaced and hungry.

Julius' Death

Maximilian had no way of knowing that his own father had left his monastery and was engaged in the war, too. Julius Kolbe had been fighting as an officer in the Polish army. He was captured by Russian soldiers, who discovered a Russian passport in his pocket. Julius desperately explained that the area of Poland he came from was still under Russian rule, but his captors refused to listen. They hanged him as a spy. Maximilian's older brother, Francis, left the Franciscan Order to join the Polish Liberation Movement. He was wounded in his service as an intelligence officer.

Following the Armistice in 1918, Francis decided not to return to the religious life. He married and later had one child. He died in 1943 in a German concentration camp.

Maximilian Is Ordained

Six months before the end of World War I, Maximilian's long-awaited ordination finally took place. It was a beautiful day, April 28, 1918, when the row of candidates for ordination lay prostrate on the marble floor of the Church of Saint Andrew of the Valley. Maximilian was ordained by Cardinal Pomili, promising to devote his life in service to God as a priest. The following day he said his first mass in San Andre della Frate.

Seeing the look of innocence and love on Maximilian's face as he elevated the host for the first time, his friends witnessed the great spirituality within him. One friend exclaimed, "This man is truly a young saint!"

But even before these major events in his life, Fr. Maximilian had added another vow: To honor and serve the Blessed Virgin Mary as long as he lived. He had already envisioned how he would do this.

The Militia Is Formed

One evening in October a year before his ordination, Maximilian called together six of his closest friends at the Franciscan college. He laid before them a plan to organize into a group to be called the Militia or Knights of the Immaculate. The rules were written in pencil on a piece of scratch paper. The seven members were to dedicate themselves to winning souls for Mary through example and prayer. As a sign of their commitment, they were to wear the Miraculous Medal.

Maximilian stayed on in Rome to complete work on his doctorate in philosophy in 1915, and in 1919 he received his doctorate of theology degree. Now he had more time to get his organization under way. He drew up a constitution and rules for the new Militia showing them to the Father General of the worldwide Franciscan Order for his approval. He then asked for and received Pope Benedict XV's blessing on his Knights of the Immaculate.

New Goals

The first part of the constitution explained its purpose: To pursue the conversion of every soul living in sin, heresy or schism, in particular members of Freemasonry (at that time violently opposed to everything Catholic). It also promoted the growth of holiness in all of the faithful under the sponsorship of the Blessed Virgin.

This was a tall order for a handful of dedicated young men just out of the seminary. But in time, much of it really happened. The Knights of the Immaculate spread all over the world. Today there are three million members.

Later in Cracow, Fr. Maximilian wrote a list of goals for his life. Among them he penciled, "I wish to be a saint, and a great saint." His teachers and many of his friends somehow knew he would get his wish. They could almost feel holiness flowing out of him as a sort of unction from another world.

CHAPTER THREE

A Prayer Is Answered

Maximilian Goes Home

Fr. Maximilian Kolbe, O.F.M. Conventual, Doctor of Philosophy, Doctor of Theology, was finally going home. He looked forward to putting all those years of study to good use. As the train rattled over the Italian hills, the young priest pulled at his tight new collar. Then, fingering the large rosary beads hanging from his belt, he gazed out the window, wondering what his future held.

Would he be sent to some distant country where he could share the gospel with the heathen? How many souls could he win for his beloved Mary Immaculate?

But on his arrival in Cracow, the Superior presented the ardent new priest with an entirely different agenda. Poland had experienced some of the worst damage of the war. Entire towns had been demolished. Homeless families and unemployed veterans wandered the countryside, without food or hope. Inflation made the few available goods or groceries too expensive to buy.

To make matters worse, a deadly influenza had swept across Europe, killing as many victims as the war had done. Many of the friars in the Cracow monastery were struck down by the deadly flu.

On his return, Fr. Maximilian was assigned to teach at the seminary. His dream of being a missionary was put off. Instead, he had to teach courses in church history and religion to the young men of the seminary.

Tuberculosis Strikes

Several times while in Italy, Maximilian had coughed up blood. He even collapsed while on vacation. He was diagnosed as having tuberculosis.

The shortage of coal in Poland made the monastery buildings even damper and cooler than usual. His disease worsened. Sometimes he shook with fever. Spells of weakness made Maximilian walk and talk slowly and perform his duties at a snail's pace.

Each day he became sicker and weaker. Tuberculosis damaged Maximilian's lungs so severely that he could only teach in a whisper. Students complained that they could not hear him.

The Superior saw that without proper treatment, Fr. Maximilian might die. In the early 1920s, there were no drugs to cure tuberculosis. Patients were sent away to dry mountain areas and forced to lie quietly in bed, usually outdoors.

Zakopane

Maximilian was sent to a sanitarium in Zakopane, a resort high in the snow-capped Tatras Mountains. Located several hours south of Cracow, it provided fresh air and beautiful views. Cracow was heavily polluted by coal used for heating and by smoke from its many factories.

Naturally, Fr. Maximilian found it hard to lie around and do nothing as ordered. He spent any time allowed out of bed helping other patients. When he was a bit better, he organized religion classes for the sick students, said mass, and offered encouragement to the hopeless.

There were many unbelievers, including some Communists, in the hospital. He converted several of them. He even baptized a young Jewish student on his deathbed. When the boy's mother came to take her son's body home for the funeral, she was furious. By becoming a Catholic, her son could not be buried in the cemetery of his ancestors.

Sometimes Fr. Maximilian visited other nearby sanitariums. On arriving, he would greet the patients and nurses, saying, "May the Virgin Mary come to your aid." Everyone loved his visits. He lost no time in inviting his new friends, both patients and nurses, to join the Militia of the Immaculate. Sr. Felicitas, a patient at the hospital, said of this dedicated priest, "When he said mass for us, he gave the impression of being in direct touch with God. Just watching him at the altar made you aware of his sanctity."

A New Idea

After two years of treatment, Maximilian was well enough to go back to the monastery at Cracow. One month after returning, with all that stored-up energy, Fr. Maximilian had an inspiration. Radio and the movies had become important parts of people's lives. Communication was the wave of the future, and since Catholics needed a way to receive information that interested them, he would start printing a newspaper. Later, he might even try producing religious films.

He planned for the friars to write and publish the paper themselves. He even chose a name, The Knight of the Immaculate. He had thought of himself as the Virgin's knight errant, born to love and serve her.

At first the friars laughed at his idea. "Fr. Max," they taunted, "what about your vow of poverty? Where do you plan to get the money? Do you expect it will float down from heaven? Anyway, we have no press to print such a paper."

The Superior stood by Maximilian, saying, "Brothers, Brothers! It is not Christian to make fun of your fellow friar. He is sincere in his desire to spread God's word." Then he turned to the embarrassed Maximilian, who had said nothing in reprisal. "Fr. Maximilian, I'm afraid we have no money to get this started. You will have to raise the funds yourself. But at least we can pray for your project."

That was enough for this valiant knight of Mary. He remembered that St. Francis had sent out his first friars to beg for their food. Swallowing his pride, Fr. Maximilian walked through Cracow's neighborhoods begging priests and nuns for donations. When he explained that he planned to use the money to honor the Virgin Mary, many gladly pressed a zloty or two into his hand. By the end of the week, he had enough money to print the first issue.

Starting **The Knight**

Father Maximilian sat down and composed column after column for his paper. As there was no press at the monastery, he took the copy to a nearby printer. Soon he had run up a big bill for supplies, paper and printing, and the Superior wasn't happy about the monastery getting into debt.

"Maybe if we had a press of our own, we could save money," suggested Fr. Maximilian. That idea wasn't well received either. Printing presses were terribly expensive. But one day a friar from the United States came to visit them. When he heard of the new newspaper and its financial trials, he gave Fr. Maximilian one hundred dollars. "This isn't much," he said, "but you can use it for a down payment."

Maximilian Gets a Printing Press

Then Maximilian learned that the Sisters of Mercy were getting a big new printing press and were looking for someone to buy their old one. The first issue of *The Knight* came off that press on January 12, 1922. It was directed to the many members of the Militia of the Immaculate. The paper was a way of holding all the members of different ages and backgrounds together. They loved it. As the Militia grew, the paper did too. Five thousand copies were printed each month. However, the friars missed their peace and quiet. They grumbled about all the commotion and the clanking of the press.

The work of writing, editing and distributing *The Knight* took its toll. One morning Maximilian woke up to find his sheets drenched with blood. He had coughed it up during the night.

The Grodno Friary

The Father Superior decided to transfer the delicate friar to a small friary in Grodno. It was in eastern Poland, in a country area which had a much healthier climate than Cracow's. There Maximilian's life took a decided upward turn. In the Grodno friary he met Brother Albert who had been a printer before entering the Franciscan Order and knew all about the publishing business. Even better, he had experience in hand-setting type and operating various presses. Fr. Maximilian bought an old printing press that was ancient and rusted. Even worse, it had to be cranked by hand. The Father Superior loaned Maximilian several friars to help with the newspaper and offered him three rooms to work in—one for writing the copy, one for the press, and another to use as a mailroom for packaging and shipping the monthly issues.

The Knight *Is Published*

It took seven revolutions of the wheel of the press to print each page of the five thousand copies. One friar worked the treadle while two others turned the balky wheel. Everyone ended up with blisters and bloodied palms from the hard work. But gradually, *The Knight of the Immaculate* began to pay its way. Fr. Maximilian wrote in a style that appealed to clergy and lay people alike.

Maximilian's younger brother, Fr. Alphonse, was transferred to Grodno to help with the newspaper. He turned out to be an excellent writer. But best of all he knew how to operate a camera. One day Fr. Alphonse strolled around taking photographs of the friars at work. He snapped them manning the press, addressing the issues and stacking them to ship all over Poland. The pictures turned out so well that Fr. Maximilian decided to print them. In addition, he put an ad in each issue: "Become a Knight of Mary." He never imagined what would happen next!

Hundreds of young men read the ad and saw the photos. Many Catholics in their teens had considered a religious vocation, but the thought of so much praying and fasting discouraged most of them. When the readers saw the photos of busy, happy friars at Grodno doing something so modern and useful, they decided to visit and see what it was all about. Many of them decided to stay and be a part of this exciting venture. They asked to join the Order, and soon the small friary at Grodno was bursting at the seams. Using the new postulants in shifts, the presses were able to crank out more and more issues.

Peace and Quiet?

One morning a snowy-haired friar peeked into Fr. Kolbe's busy, messy office. Fr. Maximilian looked up over his wire-rimmed glasses. In the next room the ancient press was making its usual clanks and groans as one printed page came off at a time.

"Fr. Maximilian," complained the old friar, "I've been hearing that awful clatter twenty-four hours a day. Can't you do anything to quiet your press. Besides, everywhere in the friary there are noisy young fellows. I entered this Order to have peace and quiet."

The busy editor turned a gentle smile on the inquirer and replied, "I can't help the racket. It's an old press. If only we had newer equipment! If God would provide a better, modern press, think what we could do for our Blessed Mother!"

"Well," added the old friar, "I hope he sends it somewhere else and all this commotion too."

Fr. Maximilian realized that the friary was getting overcrowded. They needed more than a new press. They needed larger quarters.

Fun and Jokes, Too

Life at the friary wasn't all work and no play. During recreation, Fr. Maximilian often lifted the young postulants' spirits with a joke. "Have I told you the one about the absent-minded professor?" he would ask, his bright eyes twinkling. The older friars would let out a groan; they had heard all his jokes. But the postulants urged him on, glad to have a laugh. Then Fr. Maximilian would start the story, his head cocked to one side mischievously.

"The old professor was reading," he began, "when his servant brought him a fish for lunch. After turning several pages of his book, the professor finally felt hungry. Closing the book, he marked the place with his fish. Then he called for his servant, asking him, 'Where's my lunch?'

"The servant replied, 'I'm afraid it's reading your book, sir.'"

Of course, everyone laughed loudly while Fr. Maximilian sat back enjoying the light moment.

Publishing the paper was just one of Fr. Maximilian's duties. He was asked to celebrate mass at the small country school in Losona. Twice a week he walked to the school a few miles away. When the children saw him approaching in his black robe, they jumped up and down with glee for they all loved him. Fr. Maximilian took advantage of this by inviting them to be junior members of his Militia. An agnostic teacher at the school said of him, "If all Christians were like Fr. Maximilian, even I could believe in God."

This gentle priest had the capacity to move the hardest hearts and change the character of the most fallen.

Growing Pains

As *The Knight of the Immaculate* became better known and its circulation climbed, the friary was getting more and more crowded. Fr. Maximilian said of their Grodno monastery, "The walls here have become too narrow." Obviously, Fr. Maximilian and his paper had outgrown Grodno. But, always the optimist, Fr. Maximilian would tell the friars, "Someday Our Immaculate Mother will find us a better place to print our paper." A few months later, she did. *The Knight of the Immaculate* had a home of its own.

Next to a forest in Teresin, a farming community outside the great city of Warsaw, stood a large plot of land owned by Prince Jan Drucki-Lubecki. The main rail line between Warsaw and Poznan passed right through the property. It was the perfect spot to build a new monastery and the printing plant for Maximilian's growing newspaper.

The Prince and the Friar

One day Fr. Maximilian telephoned to make an appointment with the wealthy prince. They decided to meet at a spot on the vast property. The elegant prince arrived in his chauffeured black limousine. He was dressed in a tweed riding habit and wore high leather boots. The two sat on a bench discussing the terms. Neither dreamed that a great city would soon rise on that marshy parcel of farmland.

Glancing around at the long rows planted with carrots, Fr. Maximilian imagined a series of buildings housing his religious publications and the many black-robed friars who would live there.

"How much are you asking for your property?" Fr. Maximilian asked shyly.

"My realtor recommends that I not sell it for less than a million zlotys," replied the prince grimly.

"One million!" cried Fr. Maximilian, his smile suddenly gone. In a state of shock, his wide black hat fell to the ground. As he bent to pick it up, Maximilian imagined what the Superior General would say when he heard the price: "Impossible! Forget the whole idea!"

But for Fr. Kolbe, nothing was impossible—not with the help of his beloved Mary Immaculate. "There must be a way," he thought. He said goodbye to the prince, and they parted.

The Virgin Mary Helps

That night he prayed zealously to the Virgin of Czestochowa to work one of her miracles. Naturally, the prince had quickly realized that the deal could never go through. The friars were in no position to buy such a large, expensive piece of land. But he did care about them and he was a member of the Militia of the Immaculate.

Kneeling before the statue he kept in his cell, Maximilian begged in prayer, "Help me, Most Blessed Mother. My greatest desire is to bring you honor. If you give us a place to grow, think how many newspapers we can print and how many souls we will win for your Son. Now, I beg of you, show me what to do next to acquire that land."

The statue seemed to move. Was she trying to tell Maximilian something? But what? Then an idea flashed through his mind. Perhaps Mary planted his brilliant idea. It was something so sweet, so childlike—but it might be the answer.

The next day he drove to Teresin. Walking into the neat fields, he placed his statue of the Virgin of Czestochowa in the furrows. Then standing there, his hands all brown with the rich soil, Fr. Kolbe prayed, "Holy Mother of God, I claim this land for you. And I trust that you will see to it that we build our new monastery here."

A Miraculous Gift

A few days later the prince met with his realtor. They decided to drive out to the country together and inspect the plot. Pointing to something in the furrow, the puzzled realtor asked, "What is that statue doing on the ground?"

"I guess Fr. Maximilian must have placed it there," stated Prince Lubecki. "He really wants this place very much." Then, gazing around at the woods, fields and rich farmland, the generous prince sighed and told the realtor, "It would be cruel to disappoint a priest with such faith. Go ahead and draw up the papers. Transfer my property to the friars. I know they will put it to better use than I ever could."

The realtor was speechless but he did as ordered. Later Prince Drucki-Lubecki told Fr. Maximilian that the land was his to build on. "Do whatever you wish with it," he informed the astonished priest. The happy friar effusively thanked the generous nobleman, but inwardly he offered thanks to Mary, who had graciously answered his prayer.

On a bright September day in 1927, Fr. Maximilian and four lay brothers arrived by train from Grodno to look over their new property.

A nearby family kindly offered to let the friars stay at their farmhouse until a shelter of some kind could be built for their use. Fr. Maximilian sent to Grodno for the youngest, huskiest friars to build it. They began chopping down the trees bordering the prince's former estate. A new city was about to rise on his former farmland.

CHAPTER FOUR

A City for Mary

Construction Begins

The first building constructed at the site was the chapel. Made of rough boards, it was a long, plain room seating a hundred worshipers. Next to the altar stood the statue of Mary that had brought the friars their new property. Many local farmers helped the friars build the chapel and then joined them at mass on Sundays. The solemn dedication of Niepokalanow took place on July 12, 1927.

Once the chapel was ready, the friars hammered together a wooden shack covered with cardboard and tar paper. The first brothers to move there in December slept on straw pallets on the floor, and they ate their meals on boards laid across suitcases.

When a new friar complained about the austerities, Fr. Maximilian showed him a pallet behind the stove. "This is where I sleep," he explained to the embarrassed postulant.

When newcomers were shocked at the simple living conditions, Fr. Maximilian told them, "If you don't fit in here and feel that this life is not for you, just tell me. You are free to leave at any time." Most stayed.

The Simple Life

Even if life was difficult and the work hard, the young friars enjoyed being part of something new and successful. By the end of 1929, fifty novices crowded the community. Fr. Maximilian named it Niepokalanow, "Marytown, the City of the Immaculate."

With more men arriving daily, construction never stopped. Throughout the warm summer months, husky young friars clambered over the framework of new dormitories, sawing and hammering. Of top priority was the construction of housing for the printing presses. From a distance, the friars in their long black robes looked like a colony of ants. Streets were laid and soon two-story frame dormitories lined both sides.

Even with continuous expansion, there were still no comforts or luxuries for anyone. Some friars cooked the meals in huge pots; others washed mountains of laundry in steamy tubs. Fr. Maximilian insisted that the hard-working friars receive plenty of good, nourishing food. He told them, "The car that isn't gassed up soon comes to a stop."

Many large donations came in for the new city. Fr. Maximilian used them to buy the best modern equipment for his newspaper. Soon, huge automatic presses were rumbling day and night spewing out reams of newsprint. The circulation of *The Knight of the Immaculate* had grown to 150,000.

A Great Success

The more that people heard about the City of the Immaculate, the faster it grew. The more hands there were to work the complex presses and fold and mail the monthly copies, the more papers could be printed. So much mail was received—about 750,000 pieces a week, that eight men had to be assigned just to open and answer it.

A spur of the railroad to Warsaw was built on the property. Freight cars waited on the siding to be filled with bundles of issues. They were shipped all over Poland. Fr. Kolbe was fluent in Polish, German, Italian, and Latin. He decided to publish *The Knight* in many languages. He put a map of Europe on the wall of his office, and each time the paper expanded to a new country, he stuck a pin there to mark it on the map. Mary was showering blessings on her new city.

A few times, Maximilian's mother took the train from Cracow to visit her Franciscan sons. Women were not permitted in the monastery, so she stayed at the nearby home of friends. Fr. Kolbe would drop by to visit with her. When Maria saw the sprawling city her son had built on the former carrot farm, her heart swelled with pride. But pride was something Fr. Maximilian never experienced himself. He appeared to be without any, giving all the glory to Mary, or to other workers. Everyone—princes, priests and peasants—loved the gentle, smiling friar.

Tuberculosis Strikes Again

Eventually, so much work and responsibility wore out the frail priest. He suffered a relapse of his former case of tuberculosis. Fr. Cornel, Superior of the main monastery in Cracow, sent Maximilian back to the sanitarium. He remained at Zakopane another seven months. Meanwhile his younger brother, Fr. Alphonse, was put in charge of the paper.

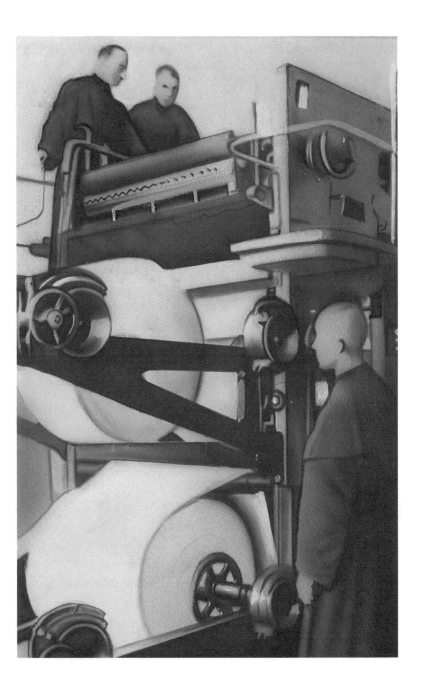

Fr. Maximilian was told not to think about work while at Zakopane, but rather to rest and relax to speed his recovery. When his brother wrote asking for advice, Fr. Maximilian would obediently reply by mail: "I am not supposed to get involved. Ask the Immaculate Mother for help. She will provide all that you need."

After seven months of rest, Fr. Maximilian was allowed to return to Niepokalanow. The doctors told him not to do any work for a year. He was to enjoy a life of leisure, with plenty of food and sleep. They even prescribed that he take a daily nap in a deck chair.

The World's Largest Friary

The doctor would have been shocked to see how much work the ill friar did every day. There was no stopping him or the growth of his City of Mary. Men came daily to the gate asking to be admitted to the Order. By 1937 Niepakalanow had become the largest friary in the world. As many as seven hundred men lived and worked there, and *The Knight* reached a circulation of 750,000.

Other papers and magazines were printed at Niepokalanow, too. Some were for children, others for youths. There was even a section on sports. The place had become so large that the friars published a weekly paper, *The Echo Niepokalanow*, just for themselves.

Everywhere in Marytown the air was filled with the acrid smell of printer's ink and the whir of presses running day and night. But the business of a publishing empire was not what spurred Fr. Maximilian and the friars. They spent three hours daily in prayer. Meditations and counseling were given and daily masses were celebrated in the huge chapel which now was a block long in order to house all the friars. Nothing was done to glorify themselves, but, as Maximilian reminded them every day, "All must be for Mary."

The buildings were simple wood frame structures. Each man had a specific job that was related to his interest and talent. Some were carpenters, others plumbers, electricians, mechanics, and, of course, writers and printers. Priests and friars were treated alike, everyone using tin plates and cups for eating and drinking.

A Job for Everyone

Even if their lives were simple, all the friars at Niepokalanow were happy as they combined work with prayer.

Once a friar asked Fr. Maximilian, "What must we do to continue progressing in our work here?"

The priest, his hair already thinning, replied, "Our outside activities are not what matters. Whether our magazines and newspapers are a success or failure is unimportant. We could be dispersed like leaves in a summer wind, but if the ideal of love and service to God and his Blessed Mother were to grow in our hearts, then, my little children, we can say that we have seen great progress."

Other frame dormitories had to be built for novices and another for postulants, as more and more young men knocked at the gate to be admitted. In 1929, Fr. Kolbe also founded the Little Mission Seminary at Niepokalanow to prepare young men for the mission field.

Several of the strongest were assigned jobs as firemen to protect the acres of wooden buildings. Wearing long black robes, and donning helmets and hatchets, over the shriek of the siren and the clanging bell they would shout, "Look out! Here come the Knights of the Immaculate!"

A Loving Father

Tuberculosis had destroyed part of Fr. Maxiumilian's lungs. One lung couldn't function at all, yet he worked harder than anyone. His door was always open for any student or friar with a problem, and he was the last to go to bed. He never asked anything special for his health, and the bitter Warsaw winters only made his condition worse. Many times he was so weak that he had to walk with a cane.

Even though he had no concern about his own health, Fr. Kolbe made certain that the men had lots of good, nourishing food. There was an infirmary on the grounds, and Fr. Maximilian visited there during recreation to comfort any sick patients.

Above all, he wanted to see his friars happy. On one occasion he said to a new recruit, "Come, my boy, you must be quite tired and hungry after your long journey. I know you will be happy here if you will love Mary Immaculate and keep close to her heart." In later years, friars who had been at Niepokalanow in their youth remembered Fr. Kolbe with true veneration. One said, "I believe that no mother ever loved her children as tenderly as Fr. Maximilian loved us."

Fr. Maximilian Meets Japanese Students

However, all this success in Poland could never satisfy a man like Fr. Maximilian. He wanted to spread his Militia of the Immaculate and the newspaper all over the world. But where should he start? One day in 1927, he was traveling on a train from Warsaw to Cracow when several Japanese students boarded his car and sat down in the same compartment.

The students looked at the black-robed priest in wire-rimmed glasses and thought, "What does this man do in his long black gown?" Meanwhile, Fr. Maximilian wondered if they were in Poland as exchange students, but with the language differences they had no way to communicate. Then Fr. Maximilian had an idea. He said a few words in Italian. As it turned out, that was the only western language they had in common. The priest and the students now had a way to converse while the old steam engine pulled them endless miles and miles across Poland.

When they came to a stop at Cracow, Fr. Maximilian pulled some Miraculous Medals from his pocket, giving one to each student. In exchange, they pressed little amulets of elephants into his hands.

On his return the priest hung the little mementos in his cell. From time to time his glance would fall on them. Then he would think of the Japanese students he had met on the train. "Those poor boys," he would think. "They know nothing about Jesus. If only there was a way I could travel to the other side of the world and tell people about our Lord, and what he did for mankind."

Spreading Out to the East

One day, gathering up all his courage, Fr. Maximilian knocked on the door of his Superior's office. "Come in," called a stern voice. Fr. Maximlian entered, wondering just how to word his strange request. After a silent prayer to Mary, he began, "Fr. Cornel Czupryk, I have come to ask your permission to go to Japan. I want to start another City of the Immaculate and a newspaper in Japan."

"Japan!" laughed the Superior. "You don't know a word of Japanese! How can you publish a newspaper in a language you know nothing about? It is very difficult and uses characters, not letters, in writing."

"Mary, the Immaculate, will provide the answer," stated Fr. Maximilian with confidence. "I am not concerned with those problems."

"So, where will you get the funds for this venture? Has someone left us a fortune I haven't heard about?"

"No, Father," Maximilian replied meekly. "I don't have a zloty." This, of course, was true. The editor of the largest Catholic paper in Poland had taken a vow of poverty. He didn't even own the patched clothes on his back.

"Well, then, whom do you know in Japan to help you? Where will you stay?" asked the concerned Superior.

"Father, I really have no idea. I am only requesting your permission. I know the Holy Mother will take care of the details." Fr. Maximilian stood patiently awaiting a reply.

Fr. Kolbe Gets Permission

Fr. Czupryk knew what a gigantic task the energetic friar had accomplished already. With a faith like his, and God's help, perhaps Maximilian could produce another miracle in Japan. But the Superior said, "My hands are tied. I suggest that you go to Rome and get permission from the Minister General. He might be able to spare some funds to send you."

In 1930, Fr. Maximilian left his successful City of Mary and took the train to Italy. In Rome he explained to the Minister General what he hoped to accomplish in Japan. To his surprise, the Superior granted him permission.

Four friars were to accompany Fr. Kolbe on the new venture, including his master typesetter, Brother John Dagis. To get to Japan the friars traveled by rail to Marseilles where they boarded a steamer headed for the Orient. They bought the cheapest tickets for the seven-week voyage, leaving Poland on February 26, 1930.

The ship sailed to Egypt, passing through the Suez Canal into the Red Sea. It continued down the Indian Ocean and across the China Sea to Shanghai. Several of the friars were seasick and wished they had never left home. At last they arrived in Nagasaki, eager to start their new ministry.

CHAPTER FIVE

IN JAPAN

A Visit with the Bishop

Upon arriving April 24, the friars' first stop was to visit the bishop of Nagasaki. In this city of a quarter million inhabitants, there were enough Catholics to warrant a bishop. Bishop Juanarius Hayasaka was a native of Japan, but he spoke several languages. Fr. Kolbe explained to him that they had come all this way to publish a Catholic newspaper.

The puzzled bishop smiled as he asked, "My dear Father, can any of you speak our language? What do you know about our Japanese people? Besides," he glanced at the friars' worn habits, "how will you finance such a publication?" The bishop knew perfectly well that Franciscans take a vow of poverty. These friars had obviously arrived in Japan with nothing.

Fr. Maximilian expressed his usual faith. "Your Grace, I expect to build a city here where we will write and print our paper."

"A city! Father, I hope you don't expect my diocese to support your venture!"

"Oh, no, sir," explained Maximilian, pushing up his

eyeglasses after bowing before the confused prelate. "Our Immaculate Mother will provide whatever we need. I am only requesting your permission."

Bishop Hayasaka was amazed to hear such faith. He raised a delicate hand and replied: "First you must find a place to live. By the way, Fr. Maximilian, I understand you have a doctorate in philosophy. It just happens we have an opening for a professor of philosophy at our diocesan seminary. Would you consider taking it?"

"Why certainly, Your Grace," exclaimed Maximilian. "It would be privilege!" Now at least they would have a permanent income. Then, bowing to the bishop again, the friars asked to be excused.

"Just a minute, Father," said the bishop. "What can these other friars do here to earn a living?"

"My brothers will be helping with the newspaper. I expect to have the first issue ready in a month."

"In that case, please," concluded the tiny Japanese bishop, "have them learn our language."

The friar thanked Bishop Hayasaka for his kindness, bowed again, and left.

A Place To Live

Fr. Maximilian had a bit of money left from their journey, and he used it to rent a small shack not far from the seminary. When winter came, snow blew in through the roof and every morning the friars had to break the ice on their wash basins. To reach the seminary where he taught, Fr. Maximilian had to climb a steep hill on foot. The friars wondered how long his frail health could take such hardships.

But he had another hardship to bear. On leaving for Japan,

Fr. Kolbe had put his brother, Fr. Alphonse, in charge of all the publications. A few months later, Fr. Alphonse died of a ruptured appendix. He was buried in the cemetery at Niepokalanow.

Fr. Maximilian received the sad news by telegram from Niepokalanow. But his mother also wrote to tell him. She was living in Cracow with the Felician Sisters. To spare her any pain, Maximilian had left Poland without going there to say goodbye. When safely in Nagasaki, he sent her a card, saying, "You will forgive me, Mother, for not calling on you before I left. But I have been very busy with Our Lady's work. We have already published our first issue in Japanese." On receiving the card, Maria was astounded to read that he had actually printed a newspaper in such a difficult language.

The Knight *Becomes Japanese*

The bishop could hardly believe his eyes when he saw their first issue with its pages in Japanese. Holding out the newspaper he asked, "Fr. Kolbe, how did you do this?"

"You see, Your Grace," he explained, smiling, "we had some heavenly assistance. There is a Methodist minister here named Mr. Francis Yamaki who studied Italian in the seminary. I wrote my articles in Italian for him, and Mr. Yamaki translated them into his native tongue. Another Japanese gentleman, a professor at your university, did the same for articles we received in German."

"What an amazing story!" agreed the prelate. "And now that you have found a way to print your newspaper, how do you expect to distribute it? There are not enough Catholics in Nagasaki to support another Catholic publication."

Fr. Kolbe stroked his long black beard thoughtfully, then

answered, "I have a plan, but only if it is agreeable with Your Grace. Perhaps you can enclose this issue inside your diocesan paper. Then if anyone is interested, readers can order subscriptions."

The bishop agreed, and now they had overcome their greatest challenge. Of course, setting the strange Japanese characters by hand in the press had been hard, too. But nothing ever turned Fr. Kolbe or his friars from a difficult task. They just kept plugging away until they found a solution.

Several More Journeys

During his first summer there, Fr. Kolbe returned to Poland to attend the Provincial meeting in Lwow. This time he traveled by train, taking the Trans-Siberian Railroad across China and Russia.

He didn't leave Japan again until 1932, when he journeyed to India, planning to start another City of Mary there. But this never worked out. He returned to Nagasaki and redoubled his efforts in Japan.

The Garden of Mary

More and more subscriptions had come in, as well as vocations. After reading the new publication, called *Seibo No Kishi* in their own language, many Japanese Catholics first asked to join the Militia of the Immaculate. Then some came to pursue their vocations as Franciscan friars.

The little band of Polish friars had grown, and now there were among them several Japanese. Fr. Maximilian felt it was time to build another city. He chose as its site a place high above the hills of Nagasaki. That hill played an important part in Catholic history.

In 1593 Peter Baptist, a Franciscan friar, and others went as missionaries to Japan. They made so many converts that the Buddhist priests complained. In 1597, on orders of the emperor, twenty-five of the priests and their converts were crucified. They are honored and known as the Martyrs of Japan. The area where they died overlooking the city is called the Hill of the Martyrs. This is where Fr. Kolbe built his second City of Mary.

Fr. Kolbe's choice of location was almost supernatural. In 1945, to end the war, American planes dropped an atomic bomb on Nagasaki. The entire city was destroyed, but not Fr. Kolbe's Garden of the Immaculate, which survived unscathed.

Fr. Kolbe loved flowers, but the friars were too poor for such luxuries. One day, after they were settled in the new monastery, Brother John asked, "Why don't we plant some flowers here?" Fr. Kolbe shook his head. "No, John. Souls will have to be my flowers." At the time, the monastery was composed of a single wooden structure.

But later as one building went up after another, the friars added cherry trees and flowers in terraced rock gardens. It looked so lovely that they decided to name their new monastery "The Garden of the Immaculate." In time a great church was erected on the site, followed by a seminary to train more priests, most of them Japanese.

Two Kinds of Monks

In every way Fr. Kolbe was far ahead of his time. He had a broad outlook and loved everyone of every race and nationality. In addition to using the talents of the Methodist minister, he gladly entertained a delegation of Buddhist monks who were interested in his work.

One afternoon, the yellow-robed Buddhists came to visit him at the recently built Garden of the Immaculate. Fr. Kolbe entertained them in the oriental manner, as they sipped tea together cross-legged on the floor. A photo was taken of the Buddhists and friars with everyone smiling and as friendly as possible.

Change of Command

With everything going so well with the buildings and the newspaper, and with several young postulants settled in, Fr. Kolbe was very pleased that he had come to Japan. However, all that work resulted in another relapse. He became so weak that two brothers had to support him when he said mass.

Eventually, the Father Minister learned of the priest's condition. In 1933, Fr. Kolbe had to return to Poland for the regular Provincial Chapter which was held that year in Cracow. At the meeting, Fr. Cornel Czupryk was elected superior of the Japanese monastery. This took some of the burden off Fr. Kolbe's shoulders and gave him more time to carry on his apostolic activities, most of it writing for the paper. When he was too ill to stand up, he wrote and edited the paper in bed.

The Provincial Meeting

The long trip back to Poland in the crowded, rickety train did nothing to help Fr. Kolbe's weak condition. Fr. Cornel met him at the station and drove him to Niepokalanow. Nothing could have given the tired traveler a greater boost

than the sight of the statue of Mary at the monastery's entrance.

Fr. Kolbe had been gone three years. Everywhere there were new faces and additional buildings and *The Knight* had grown in circulation. How comforting to see all that had been accomplished for the Immaculate One!

Fr. Kolbe didn't have a moment to recover from his journey for he had to leave at once for the gathering of all the superiors in Cracow. One of the main subjects they were to consider was Fr. Kolbe's work in Japan. Some of the leaders considered the publishing of a Japanese newspaper pointless. The Father Minister suggested that they vote on abandoning the project altogether.

Fr. Kolbe sat quietly listening to the arguments to scrap all his hard work, after which he bowed his head and prayed to his patron, Mary the Immaculate. Hadn't she always helped him in the past? Wouldn't she come to his aid now? Nevertheless, the humble priest was prepared to accept whatever might happen. Whether things went badly or well, Fr. Kolbe always accepted the will of God. His face radiated joy and peace whatever the circumstances.

In the end, the group of superiors voted to send Fr. Kolbe back to Japan, but with Fr. Cornel Czupryk taking over the administrative duties in Nagasaki as Superior. When the final vote was taken, Fr. Kolbe's work in Japan was approved. He was free to return to Nagasaki and even expand his publishing and his Garden of Mary.

War Clouds Gather

For the next three years Fr. Kolbe continued writing, and he was also involved in teaching the new friars. Everything was going well at the Garden of Mary. By 1936 there were forty-five friars. Of these, two priests and eighteen brothers were from Poland. In addition there were four Japanese brothers, one seminarian and eighteen boys in the minor seminary (similar to junior high school).

But outside that joyful place, matters were not happy or serene. By 1936 Japan had invaded and occupied parts of China. Hitler's Nazi Germany was becoming a threat to all of Europe. War clouds loomed over most of the world when Fr. Maximilian and Fr. Cornel received orders to return to Poland for another Provincial Meeting.

Fr. Kolbe left Japan wondering if he would ever return. The Virgin had assured him that a special place was reserved for him in heaven. Even as a boy Maximilian had known that someday he would wear a martyr's crown, but when and where it would happen, he had no idea.

But he told his fellow friars, "I would like to suffer and die in a knightly manner, even to the shedding of blood, if it will hasten the day when the whole world acknowledges Mary as the Immaculate Mother of God."

CHAPTER SIX

RETURN TO NIEPOKALANOW

Elected Guardian

Soon after returning to the City of the Immaculate, Fr. Kolbe was elected its Guardian. There were then thirteen priests and two hundred and ninety-five brothers at the large community, plus fifty-six seminarians and one hundred and seventy-five students. The paper had reached a circulation of six hundred thousand. Fr. Kolbe was well known as the founder of both, but he never sought credit, shying away from any mention of all he had accomplished. He preferred to say that the success was entirely due to the Holy Mother's intercession.

After the Provincial Meeting ended, the Provincial Minister didn't want Fr. Kolbe to attempt another trip to the Orient. Naturally, the friars at Niepokalanow were delighted. They looked to him as to a father. Today there are still forty-four friars at Niepokalanow who were taught and trained in Christian virtues by that holy man. They weep just remembering how good he was.

Back in his homeland, Fr. Kolbe wanted to expand the Militia of the Immaculate to other parts of Europe. He traveled to several nearby countries, starting the Militia and an Italian edition of *The Knight*. He also began other types of magazines in Polish: one for children, another with a sports supplement. His "City" had grown so large that it had a newspaper of its own.

A Daily Newspaper and a Radio Station

For years the Polish bishops had hoped to have a daily paper for their Catholic congregations. In 1936 their dream came true when *The Little Journal* was launched. It was published in various diocesan editions filled with news about parish activities, clergy conferences and political information.

That was not all. Fr. Kolbe made use of every means of communication that the modern world provided. He started a radio station and even sent some of the friars for flying lessons while an airstrip was being built on their land.

While these innovations were taking place, Fr. Kolbe was not living in a vacuum. He knew that the situation in Germany was more alarming each day. With threats coming from Germany and Italy in the west, and Communist Russia in the east, Poles were living with enemies on every border.

People all over the world stayed close to their radios listening to the latest news. Any political change could affect the lives of millions. Fr. Kolbe began broadcasts from a special studio in the City of the Immaculate. He argued, "Why shouldn't we use this wonderful means of spreading God's word and knowledge of his will for all mankind?"

Now Catholics could listen to mass on their radios and hear sermons and instructions. But the Nazis were listening in, too, from across the border in Germany.

The innovative priest had read about the new medium of television and looked forward to using that as well, but he knew that he would have to wait until television sets were available and people could afford them. That time came long after his death. He also wanted to produce religious motion pictures, and he drew up plans for a modern studio.

Fame with Humility

There was hardly a Catholic in Poland who had not heard about this amazing priest. His name was well known throughout the country for the eleven newspapers he published, the radio programs, and for his City of the Immaculate. Niepokalanow housed seven hundred and seventy two priests, brothers and students, making it the largest Franciscan friary in the world.

All the friars there loved Fr. Kolbe, and somehow he was able to keep them happy and at peace. If two brothers got in an argument, he would ask them both to kneel down and pray until they were ready to ask one another's forgiveness.

Out of affection for their spiritual father, the friars offered to buy him a fur coat to wear during the bitterly cold Polish winters. He refused to consider it, asking them, "Do all the other friars have fur coats?" When they shook their heads, he added, "Then I can't have one either."

Fr. Kolbe Protests Nazi Evils

Everyone in Poland loved Fr. Kolbe, but the Nazis across the border did not. They had been monitoring his radio broadcasts and checking over his newspapers. The usually gentle priest was highly critical of what the German Reich had done. He spoke out against their persecution of the Jews and the many concentration camps where political prisoners were starved and tortured. He wrote that retarded children, the very old and infirm, even gypsies, were given lethal injections to rid Germany of unproductive people. While never softening his words about the Nazi atrocities, neither did he refrain from speaking out against the Communists next door.

Fr. Kolbe tried to prepare his friars for what lay ahead. In one conference with them he said, "A frightful struggle is coming. Here in Poland we can expect the worst. We need not worry, but must bravely conform our wills to the will of Mary Immaculate. The physical suffering will only help toward making us holier. We should even thank those who torment us. A soft word to hard hearts may convert them. In short, we are invincible."

Cruelty and vengeance were never part of Fr. Kolbe's nature. But neither would his conscience allow him to remain silent in the face of the heinous crimes being committed by the German Reich.

War

On September 1, 1939, German troops crossed the border into Poland. World War II had started.

One morning soon after, the friars awoke to the sound of cannons. Their beds were shaking. A brother came running to Fr. Kolbe's cell and called out: "Father! Wake up! The Germans are shelling Warsaw!" That city was only thirty-five miles away.

The priest jumped out of bed, threw on his habit, and rushed to calm the frightened students and brothers. Then a plane flew overhead, and a bomb fell on Niepokalanow.

Fr. Kolbe rushed from one building to the other, comforting the frightened friars. "Quiet, dear Brothers," he reassured them. "Don't be afraid. Our Blessed Mother will protect us!" He was right. Only one building was damaged and not a single friar was injured. But worse things lay ahead. The war had come to Niepokalanow.

During the last week of August 1939, millions of Hitler's crack troops assembled on the Polish border. They had already occupied Austria and Czechoslovakia. On the night of September 1, the vast German army crossed the border into Poland. The much smaller Polish army with fewer arms tried to hold back the Germans with guns and planes. But a month later, with almost no soldiers or ammunition left, Poland had to surrender.

A Prophecy

That was when everything in Fr. Kolbe's life changed. All his publications ceased and construction of the great, modern basilica was suspended. (It was later completed in 1956.)

Realizing what might happen to Niepokalanow, Fr. Kolbe had sent the youngest students and friars to their homes. Before they left, he warned them against drinking, smoking, and losing their purity. He added, "Some of you will never return here. As for me, I will not survive the war." After that only, thirty-eight friars remained at Niepokalanow.

Following the surrender of Poland, the Nazis began arresting all intellectuals and leaders of the country. Among their first victims were the clergy. For centuries, Poles had looked to their priests to lead them politically as well as spiritually. By removing their priests, the Nazis expected to control the Polish people. As a result, 2,647 Polish priests lost their lives in Nazi concentration camps.

Fr. Kolbe Is Arrested

On September 19, 1939, a squad of German soldiers arrived at the gates of Niepokalanow. They strutted into Fr. Kolbe's office, their heavy boots thumping on the plain wood floors. Marching through his always open door, the leader shouted at the priest, "Achtung! Are you Maximilian Kolbe, editor of *The Little Journal?*"

"Yes, I am," he responded, standing up meekly. He made no attempt to resist. Maximilian remembered how Jesus had acted when he was arrested.

"Are you the man who has written articles against our Fuhrer?"

"I may have."

"Take this traitor away," barked the commandant. "Are there any other priests here?"

"Yes," Fr. Kolbe said, adding, "But they have done nothing. I am the only one responsible for the editorials you spoke of."

"Bring the other priests here," the commandant ordered. Several soldiers left to arrest the other priests. Then the commandant ordered two guards to search Fr. Kolbe's desk for evidence. They threw his papers all over the floor, and, turning every drawer upside down, they splashed red and black ink over everything. The place was a mess. Fr. Kolbe stood meekly, saying nothing.

The Friars Transported to Amtitz

As soon as the few remaining priests and brothers were gathered in a group, they were marched to waiting trucks and driven to a prison in Warsaw. It was infamous as a place of torture and interrogation.

Fortunately, the friars did not stay there. They were taken on trucks to Lansdorf, stopping at Czestochowa on the way. Seeing the black-robed prisoners, local Catholics threw them bread and candy. The friars had been given nothing to eat or drink. In the distance they could see the spire of Jasna Gora, the monastery of the famed Black Virgin. That sight renewed their courage and hope.

There they were joined by six hundred other prisoners and taken by train to Amtitz, an internment camp across the German border. The trip lasted several days. The friars were packed into a cattle car with nothing to eat or drink. One friar was seriously ill and begged for water.

The train stopped at a station for a while. Peering through a tiny window, Fr. Kolbe noticed a water fountain. He called through the slit, "Water! Water! Please give us some water." A soldier filled his canteen from the fountain and lifted it to the window for the suffering prisoner. A cruel railroad guard knocked it from the man's hand, spilling the cool water all over the station platform. "Don't bother," he snarled. "These Polish pigs are on their way to die."

In the Camp

Ten thousand prisoners were already interned at Amtitz. They were housed in tents of two hundred men each and surrounded by barbed wire fences. Fr. Kolbe was an inspiration to everyone in Amtitz, even his guards. He never said an unkind word about his German captors, even though they provided nothing but starvation rations for their hungry prisoners.

On October 12, Fr. Kolbe's name day (his namesake in religion was an earlier St. Maximilian), the other friars in the camp gathered outside his tent. They had nothing to offer him except their love. Instead, Fr. Kolbe gave them gifts. He broke his small ration into tiny pieces and gave each a bit to celebrate his day. In a short speech, he remarked, "When suffering is remote, we are willing to do everything. Now that it is here, let us accept it and bear it willingly for the Immaculate."

By November the bitter winter cold set in. On one occasion a friar awoke during the night with his feet exposed to the freezing air, and he saw Fr. Kolbe covering them with his own coat. Years later that same man wept whenever he recalled the saint's act of kindness.

At Amtitz everyone suffered from cold and hunger. But to anyone weaker than himself, Fr. Kolbe offered part of his own meager ration. In spite of the cold and lack of food, Fr. Kolbe miraculously stayed well.

Another Camp

In mid-November the Franciscans were put aboard a train and taken back to Poland to another camp. This one was somewhat better. It was in a former boarding school in Schildberg that had been run by the Salesian Fathers.

The German officer in charge of this camp was a Protestant. He was quite impressed by the friars, and he allowed one or two to walk into town with a pushcart to beg for food from the Polish residents. The owner of the local bakery gave the Franciscans bread and cookies.

Released

The Feast of the Immaculate Conception had always been a special day for Fr. Kolbe. At the monastery, he had marked it with a great celebration.

In 1939, the feast was even more special. This time the friars were released to go home. Several priests suggested that, now that he was free, Fr. Kolbe should escape to America or go into hiding in a convent. Prince Lubecki and some of the Catholic leaders had already gone abroad. That move saved their lives.

But Fr. Kolbe insisted on returning right away to Niepokalanow, inasmuch as he was still in charge there. He offered as his explanation: "My dearest children, I'm grateful for your concern, but I cannot take your advice. God has another plan for me."

On the way back to Teresin the friars stopped in Warsaw, and they were shocked to see the terrible damage the city had suffered from German bombings. Jews, wearing the Star of David on their sleeves, were forced to clear the rubble. Arrogant German soldiers stood everywhere, ready to shoot anyone who acted suspiciously.

Home to Niepokalanow

Arriving at the gates of Niepokalanow, Fr. Kolbe noted with sorrow that a statue of Mary lay in pieces on the ground. Dormitory windows were broken and papers from filing cabinets littered the offices. Yet, Fr. Kolbe showed no sign of being discouraged.

When he discovered that the few friars left behind had done nothing to repair the damage, he set them right to work. First the chapel was cleaned up and then the buildings and windows were repaired. Daily masses were started, and men were stationed before the holy tabernacle in shifts of six to pray for all who were suffering from the German occupation and to pray especially that peace would return to the world.

Rebuilding

As soon as the German air raids ended, other friars began trickling back to Niepokalanow. Quickly, their numbers reached three hundred, and with the wartime shortage of food, Fr. Kolbe had to think of how to feed them.

Then the Germans decided to use his City of the Immaculate as a refugee camp. They brought in three thousand refugees from Poznan, of whom fifteen hundred were Jews. Again this amazing man had an inspiration. There had been a great deal of destruction as a result of the bombing of so many businesses and factories. Since most of his friars knew how to build and repair, Fr. Kolbe set up shops at the monastery. The friars who were good mechanics repaired engines and farm machinery, as well as cars and the three presses the Germans had not bothered to take.

Those friars who were the best carpenters and masons were sent out to repair wrecked houses. With the money they earned, Fr. Kolbe was able to feed the thousands living at Niepokalanow. Life in the City of the Immaculate seemed almost back to normal.

CHAPTER SEVEN

THE OCCUPATION
OF POLAND

Germany and the Jews

Half a century later, it is hard to believe that such horrors existed as those which took place in what was considered a civilized nation. Since the early nineteenth century, Germany had been the intellectual leader of Europe. From Germany came the greatest scientists, composers, authors and, unfortunately, militarists. Germany's leaders always dreamed of conquering the world. In 1870, they launched the Franco-Prussian War, and in 1914 they began World War I, in which tens of millions died.

In 1939, German troops once again marched across Europe, invading and occupying one country after the other. But this time Germany was ruled by a madman, Adolf Hitler. Early in his rise to power, Hitler began planning to rid Germany of its Jews, calling his plan "ethnic cleansing."

Hitler blamed Jews for Germany's economic problems and forbade them to hold jobs. He first attacked Jewish professors, economists, financiers, doctors and artists. Jews were ordered to wear yellow Stars of David on their clothes to distinguish them from Aryans.

In Poland the German invaders first arrested intellectuals and political leaders. Since Catholic priests were looked up to in all matters by their congregations, they were the next to come under attack. At first Jews were crowded into ghettos. Later they were shipped to concentration camps. In January 1942, German leaders met at Wannsee, outside Berlin, to draft "The Final Solution," the declaration to murder every Jew in Europe. People with any Jewish blood were shipped off to death camps to be gassed. Most of the death camps were located in Poland. Other "undesirables," such as gypsies, old people, the retarded, the insane and the crippled, were also disposed of by injection or gas. Catholic and Protestant clergy who spoke out against such atrocities were sent to concentration camps, too, and thousands were put to death. Such too was the fate that awaited Fr. Kolbe.

Refugees Helped at Niepokalanow

Once Fr. Kolbe was safely back in Niepokalanow, he undertook the care of hordes of Polish refugees sent there by their German conquerors. As many as three thousand people a day were fed from the friars' kitchen. Before the war many good people had supported Fr. Kolbe's work with generous gifts. Now some of those same benefactors had lost their homes and businesses and were penniless. Fr. Kolbe looked after them too.

Sometimes local families were too poor to bury their dead, and the friars made caskets for them in their carpentry shop. The monastery hospital was opened to anyone in need, and the friars nursed those who were sick or injured.

Then on September 17, while the country was still reeling

from the German occupation, the Russians invaded Poland from the east. Both the Germans and the Russians killed priests and religious in the western areas of Poland. One out of four Polish priests died between 1939 and the end of the war in 1945.

Fr. Kolbe was everywhere, organizing the friars in the kitchen, managing the acres of buildings and property, and visiting the sick to pray with them. He still had to rise early for daily mass and meditation. These he never neglected.

Once a troop of German soldiers was quartered at the City of the Immaculate. Fr. Kolbe often distributed Miraculous Medals, even giving some to the German soldiers. Like Christ, he loved everyone, whether good or bad. He never condemned or judged even the Nazi invaders of his land.

Niepokalanow Falls Under Suspicion

Now that he was free, Fr. Kolbe really wanted to start publishing *The Knight* again. He wrote to the Warsaw authorities trying to get official permission. One day a member of the Gestapo came to investigate Niepokalanow. The officer reported back that the monastery was a hotbed of intrigue. He even suggested that it be closed down.

Learning of this threat to the hundreds of friars and refugees depending on him, Fr. Kolbe took the train to Warsaw. The Gestapo feared that Fr. Kolbe's talent of attracting people could allow him to start an underground movement. They suspected he might use his newspaper to rally Polish dissidents. Therefore, the Warsaw authorities refused to give their permission.

Day after day, German spies were in Niepokalanow looking for something they could report against the friars. They hunted for someone with a grudge who might turn in Fr. Kolbe; perhaps a disgruntled friar or a refugee looking for a favor. Fr. Kolbe even urged the friars to pray for his betrayer. He seemed to sense what was ahead.

Meanwhile, Fr. Kolbe continued his endless duties as the Father Guardian of the lives and souls of the three hundred friars still living there. He also had the care of several young men studying for the priesthood. The Russians had closed his seminary in Lwow since that atheistic government saw no reason for the training of more priests. Also, the Franciscan seminary in Cracow had been closed down by the Nazis.

Fr. Kolbe taught several seminarians living at Niepokalanow. In his "underground" seminary, he and the other Franciscan priests continued to instruct them. This, too, angered the Nazis.

Fr. Kolbe Keeps Busy and Cheerful

In spite of all his labors, and the dangers hovering around him, Fr. Kolbe managed to continue his smiling, cheerful ways. He told the young students stories about his years in Japan. When he was through with all his daily duties, he would then retire to his office to handle the correspondence, listen to any friars with problems or questions, and answer the constantly ringing telephone. Through everything he always managed to appear calm and in control.

By this time Fr. Kolbe's receding hair was turning gray. Since his imprisonment on starvation rations in Germany had ended, he had regained some weight. Everything appeared to be going smoothly and he thought it was a good time to make another try. He went to Warsaw again to ask the German occupiers for permission to publish *The Knight*.

The Last Issue of **The Knight**

Later a letter arrived from the District Board allowing him to publish one issue of *The Knight*. This was printed on the typographic machine which their best mechanic had repaired. Called the December/January issue, it rolled off the press on December 8, 1940. Once again something wonderful had happened on the Immaculate's special feast. Fr. Kolbe wrote his last published column for this issue. One sentence stands out, a veiled argument against the evils of Nazism. "No one can alter truth," he wrote. "What we can do, and should do, is search for truth and then serve it when we have found it."

The friars wanted to be sure this first issue since the occupation reached their subscribers. Most copies were mailed, though some were hand-carried. Everyone was happy to see the new issue. It wasn't long before Fr. Kolbe applied to publish another issue. Instead of the approval he expected, he learned that the dreaded Gestapo planned to arrest him.

Nazis Target Polish Priests

The German occupiers stepped up their plan to exterminate all Poles. Some priests, monks and lay brothers were shot on sight. When the Polish bishops asked for an explanation for this massacre, they were told, "In Poland the Church and the nation are one. It is easier to control the people by getting rid of all their clergy."

More and more priests disappeared as the Nazis began to hunt down former members of the Order. A Gestapo delegation came to Niepokalanow ordering Fr. Kolbe to give them a list of former friars. He knew what they planned to do to those who were caught. He also realized that the Nazis would be coming for him next.

The hundreds of friars depending on Fr. Kolbe were concerned. They begged him, "Please, Father, be more careful. What will become of us if they take you away?" Fr. Kolbe told them, "It will mean nothing—just the changing of the guard. Another Franciscan will take over." What they feared came even sooner than expected.

A Traitor Acts

In December, a lay brother named Gorgonio Rembicz discovered a way to make counterfeit German coins in the friary metal shop. When Fr. Kolbe discovered the illegal process, he expelled the man for endangering everyone's safety.

Gorgonio returned to his home town where the Gestapo eventually caught up with him. They held him for questioning, using an interpreter. The Nazi officers tried to get Gorgonio to admit that Fr. Kolbe had written articles condemning the German Reich. They interrogated him over and over, asking, "Didn't your superior publish a daily paper? Weren't there many political articles in it?" Gorgonio stated that laymen wrote such articles. Fr. Kolbe wrote only religious articles for *The Knight*.

Finally, the officers pushed a document written in German in front of the Polish friar to sign. Unable to read it, he put his name where the Gestapo ordered. Fr. Kolbe's fate was sealed.

Arrested Again

On the morning of February 17, 1941, the phone rang sharply. It was the gatekeeper calling to tell Fr. Kolbe that the Gestapo had arrived at Niepokalanow. While awaiting the officers' arrival, Fr Kolbe knelt down in his office and said several Hail Marys.

On the Sunday before his arrest, Fr. Maximilian had preached a homily on humility. In closing, he remarked, "The greatest grace of God and the greatest happiness of man is the ability to attest to one's ideal with his own blood." Somehow the holy priest foresaw what was ahead. He had been ready since childhood.

The phone rang again and a friar answered to be told that the men had arrived at the cloister's door. "Already!" said Fr. Kolbe, just this once appearing shaken. Then he composed himself and walked calmly outside. He greeted the five Gestapo officers with the words, "Praised be Jesus Christ!"

The leader asked, "Are you Kolbe?"

"Yes, I am," he replied.

Once again he heard the dread words, "You are under arrest." The leader read a citation accusing four other priests, and they were sent for. Then all drove off in the feared black cars. Heartbroken friars and seminarians watched from their windows as the men who taught and inspired them were taken away, most likely to their deaths.

Fr. Kolbe already knew what took place in the Nazi concentration camps. He had heard about them while in Amtitz. The most infamous was Auschwitz in southern Poland. He had seen the cattle cars traveling the rails by night. Everyone knew they were packed with Polish dissidents and undesirables. Would that be his fate? Or did an even worse death await him?

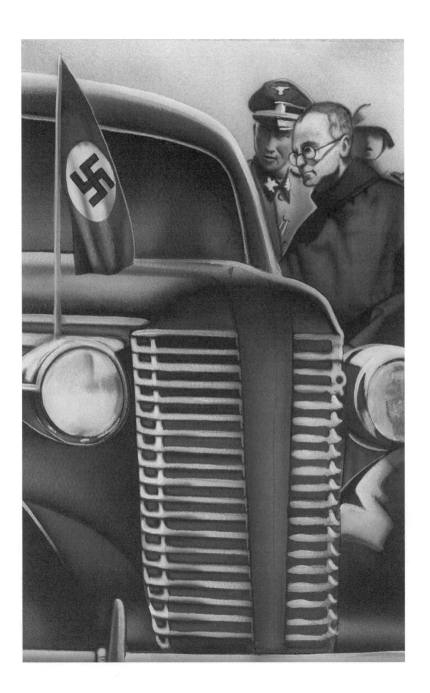

CHAPTER EIGHT

IN THE DEATH CAMP: MAY 28-AUGUST 14, 1941

The Train to Auschwitz

The freight train chugged through the pretty countryside, pulling boxcars loaded with human cargo. Many Poles knew those trains were headed for Auschwitz, the most feared of all concentration camps. Some had heard whispers of the atrocities happening there.

Fr. Kolbe was locked inside the red cattle car with another hundred unfortunate souls. The prisoners had been given nothing to eat or drink since leaving Pawiak Prison in Warsaw, where they had been held from the day of their arrest until May. Inside the train, the prisoners lay in putrid straw with only a bucket for a toilet. Some of the men were too ill from fear to use it. The stench in the dark car was frightful. Many of the condemned men wept, while others sat frozen with fear.

To lift their spirits Fr. Kolbe began singing. Soon others chimed in. From the boxcar rose hymns of praise and an occasional folk song. Fr. Kolbe moved from one prisoner to the other, praying with them and offering hope and consolation.

At last the long train jerked to a stop. The locked doors were opened and the terrified occupants were ordered to jump down on the tracks. Guards with truncheons hurried them along as snarling police dogs lunged at their heels.

The pathetic line of prisoners was marched through the gates of the infamous camp, passing under the arch on which was inscribed the words, "Work Brings Freedom." Each man feared in his heart that he would never experience freedom again. Most were right.

Fr. Kolbe Becomes Number 16670

Fr. Kolbe waited patiently in line as the prisoners were given a number. His was Number 16670. After that prisoners would only be known by their numbers. They had become faceless and nameless.

The men were handed the camp uniform, blue and white striped cotton pants and matching shirts. They were ordered to change and were given a tin plate and spoon to be worn on their belts. Without his black Franciscan habit, Fr. Kolbe could not be distinguished from any other prisoner in Auschwitz.

But word spread rapidly through the camp that the founder of Niepokalanow was there. Some knew him as the publisher of *The Knight* and the popular *The Little Journal*. "What is a man like that doing in a place like this?" they wondered.

With the attack dogs snarling at their heels and guns pointed at their heads, the new prisoners were marched to their quarters in one of the two-story brick buildings.

Auschwitz had been constructed as a military barracks when that part of Poland was under Austrian rule.

Auschwitz was surrounded by two, ten-foot-high fences laced with barbed wire. These were separated by a ten-foot no-man's-land in between. The entire length was electrified to discourage escapes and many a desperate prisoner threw himself on the wires, preferring death to torture. On either side lay a wide gravel area. Anyone who stepped there was shot instantly. A nearby wall was covered with blood where men were executed for the slightest infraction.

The guards called a halt in front of Block 18. Already crammed with six-hundred inmates, this would be Fr. Kolbe's home for the next two months. Most of the guards were hardened criminals sentenced to Auschwitz for their crimes. The more brutal they were, the better they controlled the prisoners. Several thousand inmates had been killed since the camp opened in 1940.

Friars Offer To Take Kolbe's Place

Fr. Kolbe did not come directly to Auschwitz following his arrest that February day. First the Gestapo drove him to Warsaw where he was locked in the dreaded Pawiak Prison. There he was cruelly beaten by a guard who had a special hatred for priests. As a result of the beating, which weakened him, Fr. Kolbe came down with pneumonia. He was put in the prison hospital, more a sentence of death than a place of treatment. Sick patients were allowed only half their regular rations.

Learning of their beloved leader's illness, twenty friars of Niepokalanow offered themselves as hostages in exchange for his release. Instead the Gestapo leaders were so furious that they ordered Fr. Kolbe transferred to Auschwitz.

Once in the infamous death camp, Fr. Kolbe was given no quarter. Weak and ill and having only one healthy lung, he was forced to do the same heavy labor as all the others.

Life in the Camp

Every day Fr. Kolbe marched with hundreds of prisoners to work in the fields outside the camp. Carrying hoes and rakes, they bent over the rows of stalks from early morning until dusk. Their pitiful rations were barely enough to sustain a child, much less men at hard labor. They were given one cup of imitation coffee in the morning, and weak soup and half a loaf of bread after work.

At night Fr. Kolbe would not lie down to rest. His bunk was on the second floor, near the door. He moved from bunk to bunk, saying, "I am a Catholic priest. Can I do anything for you?" Many were tormented by the thought of imminent death and he offered to hear their confessions.

There were strict rules in the camp against any kind of prayer, but Fr. Kolbe took his chances. He made the sign of the cross before eating his meager meals. At night he knelt on the floor beside his bunk to pray for others. When he was beaten by a guard, he never cried out. Instead, he prayed for his tormentor.

Fr. Kolbe Is Beaten

Under the camp's starvation rations, Fr. Kolbe grew thinner and weaker. One day, when he could barely stand, he was forced to push a heavy wheelbarrow full of gravel. It was needed to build another crematorium. Henry Sienkiewicz, a survivor of Auschwitz, later told what took place. "I could see that Father was straining hard, but unable to budge the heavy load. I stopped and offered to make the trip in his place. The guard caught us talking. First he beat us both with his whip. Then he ordered me to sit in the wheelbarrow, making Fr. Kolbe's burden even heavier. Without a word of complaint, the little priest found superhuman strength to push the wheelbarrow to the site where the crematorium was being built."

Instead of asking for Henry's help or sympathy, Fr. Kolbe said, "Henry, don't lose heart. Everything we suffer is for the Immaculate Virgin. Even here, we must pray for those who harm us."

Later, Henry was given work in a factory outside the camp. He was able to smuggle in religious medals and even hosts for communion. Mass was not allowed in the camp, but secretly one night Fr. Kolbe celebrated mass, giving the Lord's body to grateful Catholic prisoners.

In the Hospital

As the summer grew hotter, Fr. Kolbe was assigned to one of the hardest jobs: cutting reeds along the banks of the nearby river. Sergeant Krott, the cruelest guard in the camp, was in charge of the detail. On discovering that Kolbe was a priest, he ordered him to do the heaviest work and then beat him for being too slow.

One day this same guard beat Fr. Kolbe unconscious. On waking up, the priest discovered himself in the camp infirmary. Dr. Rudolph Diem, himself a Polish prisoner, was shocked at the Franciscan's condition. Fr. Kolbe was shaking with fever and suffering from chest pains. The doctor discovered the priest had pneumonia. He also recognized Fr.

Kolbe, for many times at the clinic the priest had given his place in line to someone sicker than himself.

Dr. Diem was a Lutheran of German descent whose faith had been shaken by the horrors of the camp. Sitting by the friar's bedside one day, he asked, "After living in this wretchedness, and seeing torture and death, do you still believe in God?"

"Yes, I believe," answered the ill priest. "I put all my faith in the Lord and his Immaculate Mother. Somehow, good will come of my suffering." At the martyr's canonization inquest, Dr. Diem testified, "I can say with certainty that during my four years in Auschwitz, I never saw such a sublime example of the love of God and one's neighbor."

A Fateful Day

After being released from the hospital, Fr. Kolbe was transferred to Bunker 14A. On that fateful day, July 31, 1941, several hundred prisoners were marched into the fields to harvest the crop. All around them stood guards, guns in hand, ready to shoot anyone who attempted to escape. Beside them were the ferocious dogs ready to hunt down any man foolish enough to try. The dogs panted in the heat. Saliva drooled from their fangs. What fool would make a dash for freedom against such odds? But surprisingly on that day, one desperate prisoner did. He slipped off through the hay undetected. No one noticed until the afternoon roll call.

Each morning and evening the prisoners were lined up on the assembly ground for roll call. As each man's number was called, he answered, "Here," and stepped forward.

A Prisoner Is Missing

Everyone from Bunker 14A had gone to work in the fields that day. Suddenly, there was a commotion among the guards. One prisoner was missing from the group. There had been no response although his identifying number had been called several times. Each prisoner's heart began pounding with fear. They knew what had happened before. For every person who escaped, several men in his bunker would pay with their lives. The cruel camp commander ordered ten men put to death until the escapee was found. The innocent hostages were locked into starvation cells to die of hunger and thirst. No one had ever survived this punishment.

The next day at dawn, the men were lined up again. Everyone knew what was going to happen. It had happened before when someone tried to escape. Escape was almost impossible but men who were desperate enough tried. The high walls, the sentry towers, and the electrified fences had not deterred this desperate prisoner—and he was still missing. Guards ran throughout the camp searching every bunker, and bloodhounds were set loose outside the walls.

Hour after hour passed as the exhausted, hungry prisoners stood at attention, waiting apprehensively and wondering whom Commandant Fritsch would select. As the day wore on, noon passed, and the sun burned hotter. Still they stood motionless without food or water.

Who Will Be Chosen?

Shuddering, each wondered, "Will he choose me?" Finally, the commandant ordered all the prisoners to their barracks—except for the six hundred from Bunker 14A. The afternoon heat grew unbearable. One man after another fell to the ground. Guards beat and kicked them until they struggled to their feet, or were dragged away.

After pacing back and forth repeatedly, the cruel commandant planted his shiny boots in front of the rows of trembling, skeletal forms from Bunker 14A. To him they all looked the same in their drab prison stripes, their sunken faces gray and etched with fear.

"The fugitive has not been found," he barked, snapping his heels together. "You will all pay for this! I will punish ten men from your bunker until the prisoner is found. The ten I select will be locked in Block 13 without food or water until they die."

Thy Will Be Done

Fr. Kolbe swayed, ready to fall. His head pulsed, his swollen tongue moved painfully over cracked lips, he could barely focus his eyes, and his stomach ached from the sharp hunger. But he continued to pray. "Thy will be done," he cried inwardly. "If I die, I will be with you, my beloved Mary Immaculate. I am ready to receive the red crown you promised me so long ago."

"This man!" shouted the commandant, pointing to a prisoner in the front row. "Step forward. State your number!"

"And you over there." Two choices had been made. The men stood together knowing their fate was sealed. No one had ever come out of the starvation bunker alive. As the fourth man was ordered out of the lineup, a frantic voice rose from a few rows in front of Fr. Kolbe.

"No, Commandant, please, not me." A man with a

thick peasant accent was sobbing loudly. It was Francis Gajowniczek, imprisoned for helping the Polish Resistance.

The icy-faced commandant stared unmoved, as Francis cried again. "Please, I have a wife and two children. I'll never see them again."

No Greater Love

Suddenly a frail figure broke ranks and moved toward the commandant. The guards lifted their guns ready to shoot.

Speaking in German, Fr. Kolbe said calmly, "I wish to make a request."

No one had ever approached the sadistic commandant before. "What do you want?" he growled.

"I wish to take this man's place," said Fr. Kolbe, pointing toward the sobbing Gajowniczek. The priest, looking far older than his forty-seven years, explained, "I have no family. I am old and sick. He can do more work."

The puzzled commandant asked him, "Who are you?"

Without blinking, Kolbe replied, "I am a Catholic priest."

Standing silent for a few minutes, Commandant Fritsch stared at the strange prisoner who was willing to die for another.

"Request granted," he mumbled.

Fr. Kolbe was giving his life for someone he barely knew. And Francis Gajowniczek, Prisoner Number 5659, never had a chance to thank his benefactor. But his eyes spoke the words.

The Death Cell

The ten condemned men were ordered into a line, their hearts pounding with fear. As they stumbled toward the torture chambers of Building 13, Fr. Kolbe supported a fellow prisoner who could hardly walk. Suddenly the forbidding two-story structure loomed before the quivering victims.

Passing through its steel door, they were pushed down a hall and the flight of stairs leading to the underground cells used for torture and starvation. The dazed men shuffled along the dimly lit corridor, guards striking and kicking them forward.

At the entrance to the death cell, a guard ordered them to undress. Then he shoved the naked men into the dark, forbidding cell. Their filthy, sweat-drenched garments were tossed in a pile outside. With a hollow thud, the heavy wooden door slammed shut on the helpless victims of Nazi brutality. No one would emerge alive.

CHAPTER NINE

IT IS FINISHED

Hunger and Thirst

Fr. Kolbe glanced around the dark cell. A sliver of light came from a barred window near the ceiling. There were no furnishings, only a wooden bucket in the corner for human waste.

As night fell, hunger and thirst gnawed at the men. Some wept. A few prayed. Screams and moans sifted through the door from men being tortured. Muffled cries came from the starvation cell on the other side of the wall.

Every day was the same. No food was carried in. Some men drank their own urine. Others licked moisture on the dank walls.

On the fourth day, one of the victims died. Little is known of Fr. Kolbe's final days. We offer here the report of Bruno Borgowiec whose job it was to enter the cells each day and remove the dead.

He recalled, "Each time I went to the underground cell of Fr. Kolbe and his companions, I was greeted by fervent prayers and hymns to the Holy Virgin. Fr. Maximilian would start to pray out loud. Then the others would join him.

"By the sixth day even Fr. Kolbe was too weak to sing anymore. The others lay motionless on the cement floor, but not this priest who still went from one sufferer to the next praying in a whisper. Yet a look of serenity still lit his face. The prisoners were dying fast. I had to remove a corpse each day."

On August 14, two weeks after the hostages were locked in Cell 3 of the starvation bunker, only four remained alive. Commandant Fritsch needed the cell for the next group of condemned prisoners. He sent the camp doctor to inject the dying men with carbolic acid to speed up their deaths.

Death of a Saint

As he testified at the inquiry, Dr. Bock entered the dark cell carrying the deadly syringe. In the dim light he made out three men unconscious on the floor. He placed a rubber thermostat around their arms and then plunged in the syringe. In seconds, all three were dead.

Fr. Kolbe, however, was still conscious, seated, leaning against the wall. The courageous priest looked into the face of his murderer. He smiled sweetly, as though giving the doctor his benediction and forgiveness. Then he held out his emaciated arm for the injection. That day he would wear the promised crown of martyrdom. His wait was over.

Fr. Kolbe's body was removed and on August 15, the Feast of the Assumption, his remains were dumped into the fiery oven of Auschwitz's crematorium.

In a talk during peaceful times, Fr. Kolbe had told his friars, "After my death, I hope that nothing remains of me and that the wind scatters the dust of my remains over the whole world." His wish was granted. The tall smokestack of the

crematorium belched his ashes across the Polish country-side.

One guard who witnessed the gentle friar suffering without complaint through two horrible weeks of hunger and thirst remarked, "This priest is a real man. I had never seen anyone like him here before."

Fr. Kolbe was not the only priest to die in Auschwitz. He was but one of millions of innocent people the Nazis gassed and reduced to ashes in the ovens. Farmers in the area saw clouds of thick black smoke pouring forth day and night from the tall chimneys of the crematoriums. A shovelful of ashes was all that remained of their victims, including four million Jews who were put to death there.

The World Discovers Nazi Atrocities

On January 27, 1945, Auschwitz was captured by the Russians as they pressed toward Germany from the east. At last the world learned of the frightful atrocities that had taken place inside the barbed wire fences. The handful of emaciated prisoners still alive quickly spread the word of the amazing priest who had offered his life to save another. But before that, prisoners who had been transferred to other camps and had witnessed Fr. Kolbe's incredibly unselfish act related it to other inmates. Even before the war ended, Fr. Kolbe was being called a saint.

Somehow, Francis Gajowniczek managed to survive five years of internment and starvation. Before the Russians reached Auschwitz, the Germans evacuated him and other prisoners to a camp near Berlin. At Sachenhausen, May 3, 1945, they were liberated by American troops who discovered them in a near-starved condition. Corpses of those who hadn't survived were stacked in piles throughout the camp. Fearing reprisal from the Americans, their Nazi persecutors had run off or shot themselves. Of five hundred men in Gajowniczek's group, only twenty-three remained alive. All were too weak to stand or talk.

A Sad Reunion

Following Germany's surrender, Francis somehow made his way home to Poland, arriving in Warsaw in November 1945. He had kept himself alive all those years with the dream of seeing his family again. He searched everywhere for his wife. Francis hadn't seen her, or his boys, for almost seven years. At last he discovered his wife living with her parents in Rawa Mazowiecka. Theirs was one of the few apartments still standing in that bombed-out city. "Where are my sons?" was his first sentence, once the couple had kissed and cried and hugged. Then she had to tell him.

"Francis," she sobbed, "they are gone." She fell into his arms. When she could speak again, she told him, "Our home was bombed by the Russians. Both boys were found dead in the rubble." Francis fell into a chair, shaking with grief and shock. "Why my sons?" he groaned. "Why were they taken while I was spared? Now I have nothing to live for."

Then he recalled the words Fr. Kolbe had preached to his fellow sufferers in Bunker 14A, "Accept God's will." What else could Francis do?

Soon the bereaved father found a new goal. He would spread the story of Maximilian's courageous act of love. Thousands would learn about the holy priest of Auschwitz. His incredible deed would never be forgotten, but would be an inspiration for all mankind.

Spreading the Word

After the war, everyone in Poland worked to rebuild the cities and factories bombed by the Germans and Russians. The Polish government was restored, although under Communist supervision. In time, Francis became well known as the prisoner whose life was spared through the great sacrifice of Fr. Kolbe. Many people heard the story. They asked Francis over and over what it had been like. He had a hard time describing the torture and starvation he endured in the death camps.

But when someone asked how he felt about the man who sacrificed his life for him, Francis would gladly explain: "At the moment it happened, it was hard for me to realize what was going on. We were so tired, standing at attention all those hours, and so hungry, our mouths dried up with thirst. We had been standing under the hot sun all day. I felt sad about Fr. Kolbe's horrible death. It was hard to realize I had been spared. But I made up my mind that as long as I lived, I would try to pay my debt to the holy priest. Then the immensity of Fr. Kolbe's death took hold of me. I, the condemned, would live because someone willingly offered his own life for me. Many times I lay in my bunk in our crowded barracks, wondering, 'Did I dream all this, or is it real?'"

As the days passed, Francis learned that everyone in the starvation bunker was dead. Then he thought, "I have my life because of a saint. I am determined to survive anything so I can tell the world of Fr. Kolbe's sacrifice for me."

The Story Spreads

Soon everyone in Warsaw knew the story, and Francis became renowned as the man for whom the saintly priest had died. He was elected to the Board of Commissioners in the nearby town of Brzeg where he worked as a municipal employee. In 1965 he retired. Two years later, his wife died.

Once again Francis was alone, but not for long. He traveled everywhere, making the story of his fellow prisoner's heroic death his main concern. He prayed to Maximilian Kolbe to intercede for him that he might live a long time. He wanted to tell everyone about Fr. Kolbe's virtuous life and heroic deeds, and he made plans to keep that memory alive.

A time came when the cottage where Maximilian Kolbe was born was scheduled to be torn down. Francis led the protest to save it. Members of the church where Kolbe was baptized turned the humble cottage into a museum. Francis Gajowniczek donated his collection of photos of Fr. Kolbe, as well as his letters, which he had been accumulating for years, to the little museum. Later Gajowniczek suggested a medal be struck to honor Maximilian Kolbe. Money raised by the sale of the $14 medal helped to fund Fr. Kolbe's beatification process. Testimony was taken from those who had known the saintly priest before his arrest and during his time in the death camp.

Gajowniczek's Testimony

One of the most important testimonies was that given by Francis Gajowniczek. He told the Court of Inquiry for the Cause, "I spoke with Fr. Kolbe for the first time in the middle of June 1941. We were working together pitching manure out of a ditch and we began talking. I asked him, 'Where are you from? What did you do before coming here?'

"In his prison uniform, I could not tell that the man was

a priest. But I sensed there was something different about him. He had an aura of peace and calm. He never spoke against any of our tormentors, but instead encouraged us to pray for them.

"While we were tossing spadefuls of the stinking manure into a wheelbarrow, a guard approached us. He criticized Fr. Kolbe for not working faster. By then the priest had been in the camp for several months. His body was just skin and bones. We were given only weak soup once a day, plus a chunk of bread. But he often shared his meager ration with the most frail men in our bunker. I wondered how he was able to do such heavy work at all. Many nights he coughed up blood. I knew he was not well.

"On that day, the guard again ordered Fr. Kolbe to work harder. Not satisfied, the strapping guard punched the little priest in the face. Then he ordered his dog to attack. The German shepherd jumped on Maximilian, biting his arms and legs. Fr. Kolbe accepted it all with patience and dignity. When it was over, he just returned to the ditch and continued shoveling. That night when we were back in the barracks, I asked him, 'Father, how can you take such punishment. You are an intellectual, a professor. You are not meant to do heavy labor like that?'

"Father replied, 'I put all my trust in the Virgin Mary. If you want to survive, you must pray constantly. You will persevere to the end.'"

He, of course, was right. Francis was one of a handful to survive.

Francis continued, "We were forbidden any kind of religious consolation. We were struck if we prayed. One priest who tried to celebrate mass was shot. But Fr. Kolbe, at great risk to himself, would lead groups of us in prayer. At night he would go to the bunks of other priests and friars to hear their confessions. Often he would kneel by his bunk and pray for us. All of these acts were punishable by death.

"Fr. Kolbe even gave conferences. At one of these I remember him speaking about Our Lady. His face showed the greatest love for everyone gathered around him. No matter what unpleasant work he had to do—building a crematorium, cutting reeds, shoveling manure—the saintly priest declared, 'It is all the same to me. I only desire that God's will be done.'"

The cause for the beatification of Fr. Kolbe was begun during the busy postwar years. Two more of his family had died in the interim, including Francis Kolbe, Maximilian's older brother, who had left the Order and married. During World War II he joined the Polish Resistance. In 1943, two years after his brother's sacrificial death, Francis was captured by the Germans. He was sent to Auschwitz, and later died in the Mittelbau concentration camp on January 23, 1945.

A Strange Vision

Now no one in the family remained alive except Maria. Her husband and all of her sons were dead. But on that fateful day in August 1941, as her son Maximilian lay dying in the starvation cell, she had a vision. Maria was walking down a street in Cracow when she suddenly thought of Maximilian. He had written to her from Auschwitz, so she knew where he was. In her vision, Maria saw her son lying naked in a dark cement cell. Letting out a cry, she fell in a faint to the sidewalk. Years later she learned of his death in Auschwitz. While there, Fr. Kolbe had written to her, "Dear Mother, do not worry about my health. God is everywhere and watches over all with his love." Maria died on March March 17, 1946, in the convent in Cracow where she had lived so many years.

It was during Maria's final days that the Franciscan Order put together the required papers for her son's cause. Let us hope she died knowing her son would someday be known as St. Maximilian.

CHAPTER TEN

A Saint for Poland

The Cause Is Begun

In the process by which the Church decides if someone is a saint, if the candidate was martyred, then it is sometimes automatic. Otherwise, two miracles through the candidate's intervention must be proven. The whole world knew of the voluntary martyrdom suffered by Maximilian Kolbe. However, Pope Paul VI wanted to promote his cause by establishing him as a confessor of heroic virtue. That was not hard to prove. But finding the miracles was a bit more difficult.

The cause for the beatification of Fr. Maximilian Kolbe was initiated in 1946. The Holy Office which handles these causes may take thirty years to complete it, as in the case of St. Thérèse of Lisieux, or as long as nine hundred years in the process for Duns Scotus.

The moving story of Maximilian Kolbe spread quickly all over Poland, then throughout Europe. It eventually reached and touched the entire world. It took only forty-one years from his death at Auschwitz to the ceremony in St. Peter's Square proclaiming him a saint on October 10, 1982.

There was no disputing that Maximilian's life displayed unusual holiness and virtue. His extraordinary act in offering his life to save another was heroic. But there were still the two required miracles to be documented.

Something akin to a miracle had taken place in 1945, though it was not considered in his beatification process. When Fr. Kolbe chose the site for his new city in Japan, he selected acreage high above Nagasaki on the side of a hill. The hill acted as a screen between the Garden of the Immaculate and the sprawling city below. Several people scoffed at the choice, saying it was too far from the center of activity. "Who would bother to go way up there?"

When the United States dropped the atomic bomb on Nagasaki, August 9, 1945, the entire city was leveled. Hundreds of thousands were injured and killed, and many more died later from the effects of burns and radiation. But at the Garden of Mary not a building was damaged, nor was a friar or a student injured. Mary must have given Fr. Kolbe the insight to select that place so well shielded by the hills.

After the bomb dropped, Brother Zeno, who had lived there since 1930, rushed down to the horrible scene of death and destruction. He and the other friars comforted the survivors, nursing the burned and wounded. As he watched from heaven, Fr. Kolbe must have been proud of his friars and his choice of the site—except that this master of humility was never proud, nor did he ever take credit for any of his accomplishments.

The Two Miracles

From 1945 on, several people who prayed for help to Maximilian Kolbe received a variety of healings and miracles. Two were officially approved for his beatification.

One miracle involved Luciano Ranieri, an Italian who suffered from crippling arthritis. It was so severe that the doctors had to amputate his leg. Then the wound became badly infected; he developed gangrene and was on the verge of death.

As a last resort, his family placed a photograph of Fr. Kolbe under the sick man's pillow. Hour after hour, his wife and son prayed by his bedside, invoking the help of the holy friar of Auschwitz. That night the sick man slept like a baby. He awoke the following morning completely healed.

Another miracle happened to a seamstress in Sardinia. Angela Testoni had suffered many years from tuberculosis. Her lungs and intestines had been eaten away by the fatal disease, and her family saw no hope for her recovery. Then Angela's confessor suggested that she pray to Fr. Kolbe for help. One morning her priest blessed a picture of Maximilian Kolbe and then had it placed on Angela's abdomen. That same day all pain left her and she was able to eat. Three doctors agreed that this was a miraculous cure.

Both who received miraculous healings continued to be well for many years and able to live normal lives. The cures were accepted by the Catholic Church as true miracles secured through the intercession of Maximilian Kolbe. The study into his sanctity had lasted twenty-five years.

Beatification

Now nothing prevented the proceedings. On October 17, 1971, Pope Paul VI declared that Maximilian was to be called Blessed, saying, "His name will remain among the great of all time. He fulfilled Christ's command to love one another even unto death. Blessed Maximilian Kolbe not only taught the gospel, he lived it."

Another decade passed before Blessed Maximilian's cause passed the final hurdle toward canonization, which meant Fr. Kolbe's name had been written into the canon of the mass.

Something extraordinary took place even before that special day. The newly elected Pope John Paul II was himself a Pole who had lived through the terrors of the Nazi occupation. His education for the priesthood had to be held underground to avoid arrest. He, more than any other Pontiff, could understand what his countryman had gone through.

The Pope Honors Maximilian

On June 7, 1979, Pope John Paul traveled to Auschwitz to pay homage to his martyred countryman, Maximilian Kolbe. This was not the Pope's first visit. He had been there many times before as a bishop, and then as Cardinal Wojtyla. But this visit was expressly to honor the heroic priest who gave his life.

His Holiness arrived by helicopter, landing just outside the gate of this infamous place of horror. Now a museum, it was preserved just as it appeared during the war. There were the same brick barracks surrounded by the electrified barbed wire fences. The streets were covered with the same dirt that Maximilian had walked over—except that now a red carpet had been rolled out for His Holiness.

After the helicopter landed, Pope John Paul knelt down and kissed the hallowed ground where so many had suffered and died. Thousands had come for the solemn occasion. The Holy Father quoted from John 15:13, "Greater love has no man than this, to lay down his life for his friends."

Several survivors of this death camp participated in the ceremony, in particular Francis Gajowniczek, in whose place Fr. Kolbe had died. Francis and the other former internees wore their striped prison uniforms to the ceremony.

Pope John Paul II Visits the Death Cell

Slowly and prayerfully the Pontiff walked toward the blockhouse where Blessed Maximilian and his nine companions were starved to death. The Pope was led downstairs to the underground torture cells. Entering Cell Number 3, he knelt down, his hands clasped in prayer. The remembrance of the agonies suffered by those victims of Nazi cruelty brought tears streaming down his face. Then Francis Gajowniczek stepped forward, wiping his red eyes with a handkerchief. He showed the Pope the tattooed Number 5659 still visible on his left arm.

Francis described to the journalists accompanying His Holiness what had taken place in that cell and how his life had been spared through Fr. Kolbe's sacrificial death.

Later, during an interview, Francis told the press, "Fr. Kolbe was a saint—not only because he died like a saint, but because he lived like a saint. During the weeks he lived in Block 14A with me, Fr. Kolbe was our only hope. When we felt depressed, he would smile and tell us, 'The war will end soon. You are going home.'

"Never did I see Fr. Kolbe look sad or overcome by discouragement. In his soft voice he would tell anyone in camp, 'I am a Catholic priest.' He offered to pray with all in the death camp who needed comfort—whether Christian or Jew."

Francis Gajowniczek had made his point. By 1981 nothing

stood in the way of Maximilian being proclaimed a saint by the Catholic Church.

St. Maximilian Maria Kolbe

The canonization ceremony took place on October 10, 1982, two days before the saint's name day. Two hundred thousand people crowded into St. Peter's Square to attend the beautiful and moving ceremony. Many came all the way from Poland. Some wore their colorful native costumes.

Francis Gajowniczek was seated close to the altar set up outside the great basilica. As John Paul II pronounced the words of canonization, he included the story of Francis' rescue from death. As the Pontiff read his name, Francis dabbed at his eyes. He could not contain his tears, remembering that terrible day and Maximilian's tragic death. The holy friar's gift of life filled his heart to overflowing.

His Special Virtue

The Vatican choir sang hymns of joy and doves flew overhead. A special area was reserved for bishops and cardinals of the Church in Poland. How proud they felt as the Pope recounted the heroic sacrifice of their countryman.

The Pontiff told the huge crowd, "We wish to stress the special virtue of the holy priest, Maximilian Kolbe. By the death which our Lord suffered on the cross, we have a clear sign that such love lives again in our century. Does not such a death have a special eloquence for our age? And therefore in virtue of my apostolic authority, I have decreed that henceforth Fr. Maximilian Maria Kolbe be venerated throughout the world as a martyr and a saint."

A cheer rose from the thousands assembled on that bright

October day. Then the Pope placed a scroll proclaiming the canonization in front of a framed photograph of the new saint. The picture showed him dressed, not as a prisoner, but as a Franciscan friar.

The Saint's Fame Spreads

Since the canonization the miracles have not stopped. Dozens more have been attributed to the new saint. Churches have been named for him, and books have been written about him. There are even several shrines honoring him in the United States.

During the past century thousands of Polish immigrants came to America. Most found work as coal miners, something they had done in Poland, a major coal producer of Europe.

Footedale, a small town in Pennsylvania fifty miles from Pittsburgh, is one such mining town. The Polish Catholics there attend St. Thomas Church, whose pastor is Fr. Sebastian Pajdzik.

Fr. Pajdzik served in the Polish underground during World War II. He was caught and sent to a labor camp. While there, he made the decision to become a priest. After his release, he entered the seminary and later was ordained. Even as a priest Fr. Pajdzik continued to defy political evils.

During the Communist regime in Poland, the building of churches was forbidden. But Fr. Pajdzik, ignoring the dangers, raised money to build a church in Nowa Huta near Cracow. Before that Nowa Huta was renowned as the only city in Poland without a church.

Threatened for defying his Communist rulers, the priest emigrated to America. In 1966 he was assigned to the church in Footedale. It was there that he conceived the idea of building a shrine to Maximilian Kolbe.

Building the Shrine

Margaret Todak, a parishioner at St. Thomas, recalled Fr. Pajdzik kept promising that he was going to build a shrine in honor of the Polish saint, Maximilian Kolbe. Using boulders from an abandoned mine, he would create a replica of the starvation bunker where St. Maximilian died.

Margaret laughed at the priest, telling him, "Father, you must be crazy. There is no way you can turn that pile of boulders into anything." But he did, with the help of Tony Pikulski, an unemployed coal miner. Tony spent weeks chopping down trees to form a roadbed. He and his friends rolled the heavy boulders over the log road to his pick-up truck. Using a tripod, they hoisted them up to the truck bed and to the chosen site for the shrine. Finally, a construction company loaned Tony a front-loader so that the work could be finished faster.

Every able-bodied man in the parish helped split the boulders into smaller stones to create the shrine. Completed in eight months, it has three concrete beams on the sides of the shrine to represent prison bars. Barbed wire is strung along them to remind visitors of the dreaded electrified fence of Auschwitz.

Inside the shrine is a small free-standing altar. On the rear wall a carved sculpture depicts St. Maximilian kneeling to receive the two crowns from the Virgin: the white one representing purity, the red crown signifying martyrdom.

In order to honor victims of the Nazis at Auschwitz, some of their ashes were placed inside the shrine.

Francis Visits America

Some of the men who built the shrine attended St. Maximilian's canonization. While there they met Francis Gajowniczek and invited him to come to America. They wanted to show him the shrine they had built to honor his benefactor.

In August 1983, Francis flew to Pennsylvania to visit the shrine in Footedale. By then he was eighty-three years old, his hair snow white, his face wrinkled and worn. But his blue eyes twinkled when he was greeted in Polish at the airport. On August 12, as thousands gathered around the small shrine, former Prisoner Number 5659 dedicated the medallion struck in honor of the saint who saved his life.

Francis told the reverent crowd, "Fr. Kolbe did not die in vain. He stands for the millions who were killed in Auschwitz." He continued to spread the word about St. Maximilian even into his nineties. He died on March 13, 1995, at Brzeg and was buried at Niepokalanow two days later.

He Was There

Ted Wojtkowski, a survivor who also knew the saint, lives today in Skokie, Illinois. He has dedicated his life to making Maximilian Kolbe better known in the United States.

Wojtkowski was one of the hundreds of men who were kept standing in the broiling summer sun when Commandant Fritsch selected ten men to die in the starvation cell. Ted was an eyewitness to Fr. Kolbe's loving act of self-sacrifice when he offered to take the place of Francis Gajowniczek.

Ted survived the death camp and moved to America. He became an engineer and is now retired in Skokie, Illinois.

However, the heroic act of Fr. Kolbe remained in his heart. It caused him to turn his life around and dedicate his remaining years to Jesus and his mother Mary.

Over the years Ted has gathered together a collection of mementos, books, letters and stories related to the Polish saint. In 1975 he designed a monument dedicated to St. Maximilian Kolbe for the Carmelite Fathers in Munster, Indiana. As with the shrine in Footedale, it contains ashes of those who died in Auschwitz. Perhaps mingled with them are ashes from the remains of Maximilian.

We Must Never Forget

Also still living are forty-four of the friars who studied and worked with Fr. Kolbe in Niepokalanow and Nagasaki. They contributed their memories of him to the canonization process. They still work through their preaching and writing to spread the story of St. Maximilian to all humankind.

When all of these survivors have passed on, the name of Maximilian Kolbe, the saint of Auschwitz, will help to keep their memories alive. That is most important because the incredible horrors that men have done against their fellow humans must never be forgotten. But neither must we forget the greatness that others demonstrated by their courage, self-sacrifice and faith.

During his short life of forty-seven years, Fr. Kolbe composed millions of words for his many publications, but this short sentence says it all: "My little children, remember, holiness is not a luxury, but a simple duty." St. Maximilian Kolbe performed that duty with perfect love and devotion. He is an example for all Christians everywhere.

BIBLIOGRAPHY

St. Maximilian Maria Kolbe

BEIZE, Bishop Bohdan. *Wsiety Maksymilian Werod Nas.* Lodz, Poland: 1994.

Butler's Lives of the Saints. San Francisco: Harper and Row, 1985. St. Maximilian Kolbe entry.

COPP, Jay. "Inspired by a Martyr." *Catholic Digest,* March 1995.

DELANEY, John I. St. Maximilian Kolbe entry. *Dictionary of Saints.* New York: Doubleday, 1980, p. 341.

DEWAR, Diana. *The Saint of Auschwitz, Maximilian Kolbe.* New York: Harper and Row, 1981.

ESPER, George. "Pole Visits U.S. Shrine." *Salt Lake Tribune,* September 16, 1984.

FORRISTAL, Desmond. *Kolbe: A Saint in Auschwitz.* New Rochelle, New York: Don Bosco Multimedia, Patron Books, 1983.

FRANCISCAN FRIARS OF MARYTOWN STAFF, eds. *The Hero of Auschwitz.* Libertyville, Illinois: Prow Books, 1979.

FRAZONIA, Franck. "St. Maximilian: Greater Love Had No Man." *Catholic Digest,* May 1986.

HANLEY, Boniface. *Maximilian Kolbe: No Greater Love.* Notre Dame, Indiana: Ave Maria Press, 1982.

HEINE, Marc. *Poland.* New York: Hippocrene Books, 1988.

KLUTZ, Ladislaus, O.C.D. *Kolbe and the Kommandant: Two Worlds in Collision.* Stevensville, Montana: DeSmet Foundation, 1983.

LORIT, Sergius C. *The Last Days of Maximilian Kolbe.* New York: New City Press, 1968.

McSHEFFERY, Daniel F. "Maximilian Kolbe: The Saint of Auschwitz." *Liguorian,* July 1995.

MLODOZENIEC, Juventyn M. *I Knew Saint Maximilian Kolbe.* Washington, New Jersey: AMI Press, 1983.

"New Saint." *Parade Magazine,* October 10, 1982.

RICCIARDI, Antonio. *St. Maximilian Kolbe.* Boston: St. Paul Books, 1982.

ROMB, Anselm W. *A Kolbe Reader.* Libertyville, Illinois: Prow Books, 1987.

TREECE, Patricia. *A Man for Others.* New York: Harper and Row, 1982.